Activity-Based Management for Financial Institutions

Wiley & SAS Business Series

The Wiley & SAS Business Series presents books that help senior-level managers with their critical management decisions.

Titles in the Wiley and SAS Business Series include:

For more information on any of the above titles, please visit **www.wiley.com**.

Activity-Based Management for Financial Institutions

Driving Bottom Line Results

Brent Bahnub

WILEY

John Wiley & Sons, Inc.

Published by John Wiley & Sons, Inc., Hoboken, New Jersey.
Published simultaneously in Canada.

For general information on our other products and services or for technical support, please contact our Customer Care Department within the United States at (800) 762-2974, outside the United States at (317) 572-3993 or fax (317) 572-4002.

Wiley also publishes its books in a variety of electronic formats. Some content that appears in print may not be available in electronic books. For more information about Wiley products, visit our website at www.wiley.com.

Library of Congress Cataloging-in-Publication Data

Bahnub, Brent.
 Activity-based management for financial institutions: driving bottom line results/ Brent Bahnub.
   p. cm.
 Includes index.
 ISBN 978-0-470-56222-2 (cloth)
 1. Activity-based costing. 2. Financial institutions. I. Title.
 HF5686.C8B24 2010
 332.1068'1–dc22

2009041466

Printed in the United States of America

10 9 8 7 6 5 4 3 2 1

For Jordan, Taylor, and Logan

Contents

Foreword

With this book Brent Bahnub has made an important contribution to the body of knowledge of managerial accounting by providing a comprehensive guide to the key aspects of activity-based costing—generating interest and buy-in for it, designing the system, avoiding implementation pitfalls, and applying its information for decision support and analysis to drive bottom line results. This book provides hope for those who recognize the deficiencies of their existing traditional costing methodology and system. It reveals what can now be accomplished by leveraging the progressive power of information technology that was only recently developed and mastered in the 1990s.

Have there been other books written about activity-based costing and management? Of course. I even authored a few. But the majority of material written about activity-based costing (ABC) described outcomes from before ABC software was advanced to the stage to accommodate much more flexible modeling including multi-stage cost assignments, multi-dimensional viewing, and scoring costs with attributes (like value-added versus nonvalue-added), to name a few.

Brent is proof of a hypothesis I have long held—that those who have actually experienced implementing a project or system are far more capable of explaining the concepts than those who simply research it.

THE NEED TO REPLACE TRADITIONAL COST MEASUREMENT METHODS

To provide some background, before flexible modeling with ABC principles became possible, accountants were restricted to the traditional thinking of debits and credits and departmental step-down cost allocations of support departments succeeded by 1980s primitive two-step cost allocation of work activities. With 1980s ABC thinking, accountants still continued routinely to violate the cause-and-effect principle's relationships (still using broad-brushed cost allocation factor averages, though less broad) that 21st century ABC technology enabled compliance with. Fortunately, that reluctance to adopt ABC has been gradually shifting and those who genuinely care about facilitating better decision making for their organization are embracing it.

Brent's employment in the 1990s with Ernst & Young's management consulting arm and with organizations that applied commercial ABC software gave him the opportunity to work with similarly talented professionals who were all simultaneously observing organizations that could finally discard the yoke of restrictive costing practices and truly model the transformation of resource expense inputs (e.g., salaries, supplies, travel, etc.) into their *calculated* costs, so that the costs realistically represented the economics of the organization. Costing is modeling. It was an experience for Brent similar in exhilaration to what junior architects enjoyed who worked at Frank Lloyd Wright's Talleyson, Wisconsin offices, or young scientists felt working at Thomas Edison's "idea factory." The knowledge of better ways to model costs accelerated as organizations that had purchased ABC software were applying it to their organization's real world problems.

OVERCOMING THE SPEED BUMPS OF ABC

Along ABC's bright successes in the 1990s, there also came limited results and in some cases failures. And perhaps due to misguided lofty expectations that ABC would be some form of a magic pill that could solve all problems, rumors circulated that ABC was ineffective. People still periodically ask me, "Is ABC still going on?" as if it had passed on as another short-lived management fad. The implication was that either ABC system implementations were scaling down or being abandoned—or that those organizations that had not yet implemented ABC had examined it and chosen likely not to implement it near term.

The problem was not with the principles of ABC, but rather with how it was being implemented and with how its positive impact on improved decision making was not fully appreciated. It will be tough to stop the use of ABC-principled accounting because it correctly answers eternal questions that managers will forever be asking. What do things cost? Where do we make or lose money? What will be the future impact on spending from possible planned changes?

ABC is indeed alive and well. This book provides evidence of real implementations with real significant results to prove it. Brent's book demonstrates the successful adoption of ABC.

I am honored that Brent invited me to write this Foreword for his book. The past few years I have had the privilege to present seminars all over the world on the broader topic of performance management that includes ABC, strategy maps, and balanced scorecards, and other components. As background, I was fortunate to have gotten involved with the ABC movement as a consultant with KPMG Peat Marwick in the mid-1980s and trained then by Professors Robert S. Kaplan and Robin Cooper of the Harvard Business School. Bob and Robin were pioneers in researching, documenting, and applying ABC.

Once I was exposed to the logic of and superior visibility from ABC, I wondered, "Why doesn't everybody use this practice?" But now that roughly twenty-five years have passed since ABC was formally introduced by Kaplan, I still wonder what accounts for the slower than expected adoption of ABC. In my travels I routinely ask this question of trusted practitioners in this field. The initial explanations include lack of good data or the complexity or inability for software to replicate the ABC principles. But, as I mentioned, those obstacles were resolved in the early 1990s when "end-to-end" integrated commercial ABC software had matured and ABC implementers learned to use quick ABC rapid prototyping with iterative remodeling methods to get quick results with sufficient accuracy. For example, the customers of my employer, SAS, the world's largest provider of business analytics software including an ABC offering, provide testimony that ABC is essential to their performance management and improvement.

A deeper explanation surfaced that the mentality of accountants, who often drive ABC implementation projects, may have done more damage than good for the ABC movement. That is, not only is the accountant's unnecessary concern for precision and exactness (in my experience, accountants do not actually harbor a fixation on precision and exactness for ABC) a hindrance because of the resulting oversized and overengineered ABC models that retard learning and buy-in, but their concern that their accounting data reconcile with generally accepted accounting principles (GAAP) regulatory reporting may even have been a worse obstacle.

More recently I have heard opinions about ABC's slow adoption rate that support one of the unspoken laws of management: If your senior leadership cannot articulate the basic principles of an improvement initiative, then employees will never achieve or sustain the initiative. And if the leadership is weak, success may be low. I believe this may better explain why the adoption rate of ABC has been so gradual.

But as I attend various business conferences and continue to spend time with organizations that have been using ABC for several years, I am very impressed with the depth of problems it is being used to solve. Brent's book reveals how financial service firms, including banks, have applied ABC to their back-office operations and shared services to validly measure, report, and charge back costs to departments served. The book's lessons apply to all service sector organizations and arguably also to manufacturers and distributors as they increasingly add customer services to their commodity-like products for strategic competitive differentiation.

Perhaps even more important, Brent's book also reveals how organizations are moving beyond measuring product and standard service-line profitability further to measuring customer profitability and value—treating existing and future customers as if an investment in a portfolio—in order for their sales and marketing people to better deploy resources for differentiated customer treatments and segmented marketing campaigns with varying deals and offers in proportion to the value of the customer or sales prospect. Granular ABC data is integral in those calculations.

ABC PROVIDES LIGHT AT THE END OF THE TUNNEL

So does ABC work? Sure it does. But implementers need to be prudent and economical. Any improvement initiative like ABC will always be judged by management based on a cost versus benefits test. If organizations keep the administrative effort to operate ABC low and the benefits from using the data for decision analysis high, then ABC systems will be adopted and sustained. My sense is that in the next decade or two, ABC will be as widely accepted as standard cost accounting is today.

But some hurdles that must be overcome lie ahead. Brent's book not only sheds light on what the obstacles and implementation pitfalls for ABC are but is also prescriptive on how to resolve them. It is no wonder that managers and employee teams typically do not trust their cost accounting data and continue to wait for the day that they can have visibility and transparency to the hidden costs that comprise their outputs and insights to the external forces and cost drivers that cause their expense structure. Brent's book accelerates that future day to today.

This book inspires organizations to decide to get started (or restart) rather than postpone the inevitable.

Gary Cokins

Preface

Over the past fifteen years, I have had the unique experience of seeing Activity-Based Costing/Management (ABC/M) from nearly every perspective. First, as an MBA student at Columbia Business School, I learned the high-level theory of ABC. Of course, at a high level, ABC is extremely straightforward. I wondered why every company in the world had not already moved to ABC. ABC is clearly superior to traditional costing.

Next, as a consultant working for Ernst & Young and subsequently CapGemini, I designed and implemented ABC and chargeback solutions at several Fortune 100 financial services companies. In all cases, the ABC implementations were considered successful and the consulting engagements ended prior to establishing a sustained ABM process and realizing many ABM benefits. Sure, ABM benefits were identified and some were implemented prior to the completion of the consulting engagements, but the ABM benefits never seemed to reach their full potential after we left.

Then I decided to eat my own cooking and leave the consulting world to implement ABC at National City Bank. I was determined not only to implement ABC, but also to realize much greater returns by structuring the ABM portion of the solution. However, prior to the completion of the ABC journey, I was asked to become the Chief Financial Officer for the Operations and Information Services division of National City. The opportunity was too good to let it pass. So, for the next two years, I performed the duties of the divisional CFO and continued to be a vocal advocate of ABC/M within the bank. While there were pockets of multi-million dollar savings, I still felt that we could have done better.

My epiphany occurred at the next leg in the journey. I was requested to identify and lead focused improvement efforts on a subset of assets within the bank. I was given full rein to design the opportunity identification and governance processes. I defined team member roles and selected my own team. I used the ABM and organizational change management techniques in this book to improve the business by more than $40 million annually. That was the home run I was craving!

In mid-2008, I transitioned out of ABC/M and process improvement when I became the group manager for commercial deposit products at National City. My ABC/M experience was now complete. I had moved from being the designer and implementer of ABC/M solutions to being the primary customer of ABC/M solutions. As I made the transition, I thought it would be a waste of knowledge not to document the experiences and lessons learned over the past fifteen years.

So, what was the epiphany? It was very simple, actually. ABC without ABM does not matter. The focus needs to shift away from ABC towards ABM. Here is a shocker: There is no such thing as a perfect ABC model and there never will be. If you believe that you can assign individual costs—like everyone's actual purchase price of their office personal computer—to multiple products across multiple lines of business with 100.0000% accuracy, you are sadly mistaken.

Does it matter that ABC models are not perfect? Of course not. Debates about whether ABC models are "right" or "wrong" are nonsensical. There are not "right" or "wrong" ABC models; there are just more accurate and less accurate ABC models. Across the board, ABC solutions are significantly more accurate than standard costing. Acceptable ABC models are probably more than 80% accurate. Good ABC models are probably more than 90% accurate. Business leaders should be comfortable making decisions on data that is more than 90% accurate.

Instead of saying goodbye to ABC/M forever, my passion for ABC/M was reignited while I wrote this book and I accepted a position driving ABM improvements at First Niagara Bank. Once again, I am excited at the opportunity to drive millions of dollars in value to the shareholders through ABM.

Many books have been written about Activity-Based Costing and Activity-Based Management over the past twenty years. In my experience, I found Gary Cokins' and Robert Kaplan's books particularly useful.

This book expands on existing ABC/M work in five areas:

1. **More focus on how to drive ABC data to the bottom line using ABM and other organizational change management techniques.** ABC without ABM is a waste of shareholder value. This book is not intended to teach you how to make the best ABC model. It is intended to help you actually drive bottom line results. That does not happen without ABM and strong organizational change management.

2. **Stronger focus on the financial services industry.** Originally, manufacturing undertook and, in some cases, mastered ABC/M. Most financial services firms could still drive millions of dollars of improvements through better use of ABC/M.

3. **More emphasis on shared services.** A major component of financial services is the back office. At times, the shared services organization is the initiator of ABC/M projects as a method to clearly articulate and improve its cost structure. In all cases, the shared services organization was my starting point for ABC/M.

4. **Stronger emphasis on Organizational Change Management (OCM).** OCM is a tremendous enabling discipline for process improvement. Combined with the power of the ABC data, OCM makes driving ABM value a reality.

5. **Templates, tools, and techniques to improve the odds of a successful ABC/M implementation.** Through years of leading ABC/M implementations, I have seen and used what works and what does not. This knowledge, in and of itself, will save you months of headaches and possibly your career. The templates in this book are available on the companion website (see page xix).

This book is intended to be used by people with at least a basic knowledge of ABC/M. The book provides a basic ABC/M refresher in Chapter 1, but does not dwell on introductory generic examples of ABC calculations. Although the examples in the book are primarily from the financial services industry, it should be particularly useful to any former or current ABC implementer trying to determine why the ABC/M project has not been as financially successful as it should have been. This elusive success requires a renewed focus and commitment to ABM.

While ABC/M can be a dry topic, I have tried to provide some levity throughout the book. My wit can be a bit caustic at times and although my wife frequently advised me to refrain from such comments, some still remain. To those of you easily offended, I apologize in advance. Also, like most people, I have a tendency to write the way I speak, so I apologize in advance to English majors everywhere.

As a lifelong advocate of knowledge sharing, I hope these lessons learned from driving bottom line results and leading ABC/M projects will make your life a bit easier. Best of luck in your endeavors!

About the Website

This book includes a website, which can be found at www.wiley.com/go/activity-basedmanagement. This website includes time-saving templates and samples from several chapters.

From "Implementing ABC" (Chapter 3):

- **Activity Dictionary - Spreadsheet Sample.xls.** Jumpstart your activity dictionary capture with this simple format. In addition to the basic activity capture information, the file entry of up to six tasks per activity.

From "Implementing ABM" (Chapter 4):

- **ABM Process - ABM High-Level Business Case - Template .xls.** Quantify your ABM opportunities by using this one-page business case estimate. A single year of benefits is compared to the implementation and annual costs to focus efforts on quick paybacks.
- **ABM Process - ABM Project Summary - Sample WS 010. doc.** Define your ABM opportunities by quantifying the baseline and expected measurements. Also, define "completion" for each of the initiatives instead of undertaking a never-ending journey.
- **ABM Process - Implementation Letter - Sample.ppt.** Obtain public and psychological commitment from your project champions through the use of this straightforward sample.
- **ABM Process - ABM Exception - Template.xls.** For the rare ABM exception request, be prepared with this predefined, standard exception form.

- **PPM Tool - Pair-wise Ranking Example.xls.** Use this tool to determine your project "winners" in head-to-head comparisons.

- **PPM Tool - Project Ranking Tool.xls.** Use this tool to evaluate projects based on strategic alignment, net shareholder value, implementation risk, and project duration. This is a classic project ranking tool.

- **PPM Tool - Balanced Scorecard Project Ranking.xls.** Link your ABM opportunities to balanced scorecard dimensions through the use of this tool.

From "Managing Organizational Change" (Chapter 6):

- **OCM Tool - Stakeholder Assessment Table.xls.** Assess project stakeholders based on their power, concern, knowledge, and accessibility. Use this template to determine necessary stakeholder actions.

- **OCM Tool - Stakeholder Action Plan - Template.ppt.** Based on the stakeholder assessment, document risks, mitigating actions, mitigation timing and responsibility.

- **OCM Tool - Communications Plan - Sample.ppt.** Define your ABC/M communication needs and associated actions using this simple sample.

The password to enter this site is: Bahnub.

Acknowledgments

I have been absolutely blessed with tremendous support by many people. No one person could possibly ever *earn* or *deserve* this support, so "blessed" is the best way I can describe it.

First, I owe special thanks to my wife, Jodie, for her unending support and encouragement. Because of her business insight and common sense, she has always been a tremendous sounding board. Of course, that is in addition to her being a great wife and mother. I love you, Jodie!

Thanks to Drew Doherty for his fantastic edits. His input was invaluable. We have been through a lot over the years, including the attacks on the World Trade Center in 2001. I could work with Drew my entire career and enjoy every minute—well, except for the diatribes about Yankee baseball greatness.

Thanks to Allen Friedman, my friend and consulting mentor, for years of opportunity and advice. He brings a great business mind to any situation. If I had not written this book, he could have.

Thanks to Gary Cokins for his inspiration and insightful work on ABC/M. In many ways, Gary is the godfather and torchbearer for ABC/M. I am honored that he wrote the Foreword for this book.

Thanks to Jeff Kelly for his support and advice at National City Bank. The variety of career opportunities at National City Bank has enabled me to see all aspects of ABC/M and change management.

Thanks to Mike Harrington at First Niagara Bank for his patience and support during the final editing and publishing of the book. We will do great things.

Thanks to all of the former ABC/M team members over the years. While I am sure I have forgotten a few names, this list includes: Fred Asbeck, Daria Jakubowycz, David Hertz, Natasha Steptoe, Jonathan Fikse, Solomon Dadzie, Kathy Yang, Mike Hicks, Lee Adams, Chitrang

Purani, Michelle Oden, Tom Krawiec, Kelly Adams, Steve Posch, Diana Fanchi, Lisa Giganti, Brenda O'Reilly, Tom Ford, Keri Kowalski, Janet Kapostasy, Colleen McDevitt, Appoline Mahle, Dinko Bacic, Mike Tracey, Gary Dean, Jeff Smith, and Christine Yoke.

Thanks to Sheck Cho, Helen Cho, Stacey Rivera, and the people at John Wiley & Sons for their patience, expertise, and willingness to work with me. Authoring and publishing a book is an intense process.

And last, but certainly not least, thanks and much respect to my parents, Jeff and Enid. I continue to strive to be what you always have been—intelligent, hard-working, honest, fair, caring, and loving. Truly, I have been blessed all of my life.

CHAPTER 1

What Are ABC and ABM?

The brain is a wonderful organ. It starts working the moment you get up in the morning and does not stop until you get into the office.

—Robert Frost

WHAT IS ABC?

Activity-Based Costing (ABC) is an accurate method of assigning costs to work activities, processes, products/services, customers, and lines of business. It is based on the notion that efforts required to produce products and services can be quantified and, therefore, assigned to the product or service. Similar to a bill of materials, products have a bill of activities required to deliver the product or service. For simplicity's sake, "products or services" will be referred to as "products" from this point forward, understanding the concepts apply to both.

Background

After reducing direct material and labor costs in the mid-1970s, organizations recognized that antiquated information systems were not meeting their ever-changing management information needs. Many companies embarked on ABC initiatives to focus on indirect product and service costs. By assigning overhead costs, companies were able to

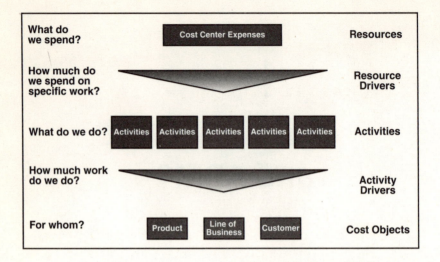

FIGURE 1.1 Basic ABC Flow and Terminology

clearly identify, improve, or divest unprofitable products, inefficient processes, and poorly performing regions.

The cornerstones of ABC are that cost is *consumed* and consumption can be managed. As such, ABC provides an excellent basis for cost accounting, chargeback, and performance management.

Figure 1.1 illustrates the flow of ABC information. The left column identifies the business questions addressed at each level. The middle column provides a visual representation of ABC implementation. The right column identifies the common ABC terminology used to describe the data.

ABC Terminology Definition

Figure 1.2 represents a simplified example of ABC cost flow for bank operations.

Using Figures 1.1 and 1.2 as references, let's further define some of the ABC terminology.

- **Resources** represent all the available means that work activities can use to provide products to Lines of Business (LOBs) and

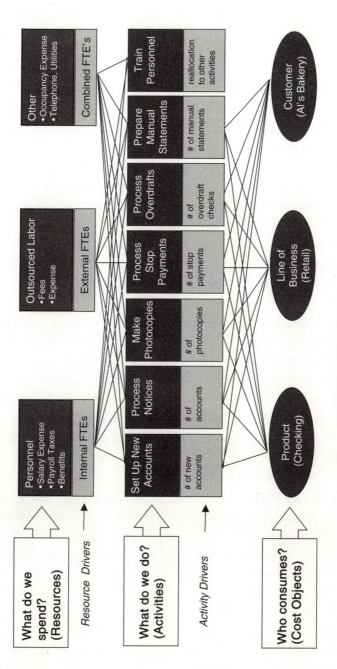

FIGURE 1.2 Simple ABC Example

3

customers. Examples of resources include personnel, equipment, third-party contracts, and facilities.

- **Resource Cost Pools** are logical groupings of resources (quantified in General Ledger accounts) that are consumed in the performance of activities. The three resource cost pools shown in Figure 1.2 are Personnel, Outsourced Labor, and Other.

- **Resource Drivers** are measurements of the resources consumed by an activity. Notice that the resource drivers in Figure 1.2 are different for each of the resource cost pools. If the resource drivers for the resource cost pools are the same, there is an opportunity to consolidate resource cost pools. This will be discussed in more detail later in the book.

- **Processes** (not shown) are groups of related and interdependent activities performed to achieve a specific objective. Within a bank, a process called "Add Funds" includes all activities required to credit a customer's deposit account.

- **Activities** are what people and systems do in an organization. Activities consume resources to produce an output. Activity names begin with a verb. Examples of activities include Set Up New Accounts, Process Notices, and Train Personnel.

- **Tasks** (not shown) are the components of an activity and tell us how activities are performed. Processes, activities, and tasks represent a logical business process model decomposition. Each process, activity, and task should start with a verb and collectively define the hierarchical level above it.

- **Activity Drivers** are measurements of the frequency and intensity of demand placed on an activity by cost objects. They are similar to resource drivers. Notice that the activity drivers in Figure 1.2 are different for each of the activities. If the activity drivers for multiple activities are the same, there is an opportunity to consolidate activities. This will be discussed in more detail later in the book.

- **Cost Objects** represent the persons or things that benefit from incurring work activities. Examples of cost objects include products, LOBs, and customers.

Company Income Statement

Loan Net Interest Income	$1,000
Loan Application Expense	300
Payments Processing Expense	400
Net Income	$ 300
Margin	30%

FIGURE 1.3 Consolidated Product Income Statement

ABC versus Traditional Costing

So, how is ABC different from traditional costing? Let's compare. Figure 1.3 shows a consolidated net income statement from a two-product company. The company receives revenue (Net Interest Income) from the two loan products it offers. The loans require resources from Application and Payments Processing.

Using traditional costing, the costs of the products are allocated based on the revenues of the products. In the example shown in Figure 1.4, Loan Product E (easy) contributes 60% of the revenue while Loan Product D (difficult) contributes 40% of the revenue.

Figure 1.4 shows the 60/40 split of expenses, resulting in a 30% margin for both products. In reality, however, the loan products are very different. Loan Product E (easy) requires a web-based application and electronic payments. Loan Product D (difficult) is a traditional paper-based application with paper check payments. If Product D's applications took five times the effort of Product E and the payments took twice the effort of Product E, the ABC results would look like Figure 1.5.

	Product Ⓔ	Product Ⓓ	Total
Loan Net Interest Income	$600	$400	$1,000
Loan Application Expense	180	120	300
Payments Processing Expense	240	160	400
Net Income	$180	$120	$ 300
Margin	30%	30%	30%

FIGURE 1.4 Traditional Product Income Statement

	Product Ⓔ	Product Ⓓ	Total
Loan Net Interest Income	$600	$400	$1,000
Loan Application Expense	50	250	300
Payments Processing Expense	133	267	400
Net Income	$417	($117)	$ 300
Margin	70%	(29%)	30%

FIGURE 1.5 ABC Product Income Statement

Notice the dramatically different margins as a result of assigning costs based on consumption rather than allocating (spreading) costs based on traditional costing. Product D is actually destroying shareholder value.

ABC Results

Activity-Based Costing has been used for decades with mixed results. Let's make sure we are on the same page regarding the definition of success: sustained improvement of shareholder value through improved cash flow. As a proxy, it is often easy to use Net Income Before Taxes (NIBT) as a "success" scorecard, knowing full well that there may be circumstances that require the demonstration of improved cash flow.

As you will see, it is very important to define success early and often for any change. Many people get personal success—the implementation of a system or process, the accolades from peers—confused with the shareholder's definition of success. This book is intended to highlight key elements of successful implementations—and, just as importantly, to help the reader avoid the numerous pitfalls before, during, and after the implementations.

Many of the examples in the book are drawn from my past implementations in shared service environments within the financial services sector—banking and insurance. It is an incredibly complex arena with many options and opinions. Since the majority of the employees working in the financial services industry are financially oriented, many believe that they could easily create an Activity-Based Costing/Management model and culture. In fact, it takes years for a costing novice to understand and incorporate all of the nuances required for a successful implementation. While a small library could be created to house ABC literature, very few of these books go into great depth regarding the methods to drive ABC to the bottom line.

WHAT IS ABM?

Activity-Based Management (ABM) is active process management undertaken to improve performance. The relationship between ABC and ABM is best depicted in Figure 1.6 and is commonly referred to as the CAM-I Cross. While ABC focuses on assigning resources to activities and activities to cost objects, ABM decomposes a business process model into activities and then to performance measures. The moniker ABC/M (Activity Based Costing/Management) is used to identify the full scope of both ABC and ABM.

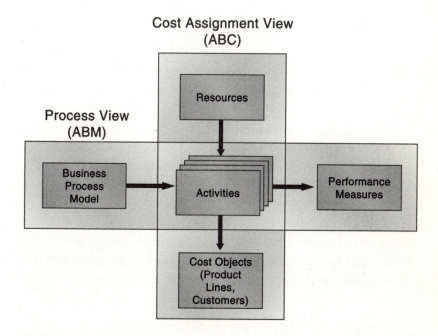

FIGURE 1.6 The CAM-I Cross

Source: The Consortium of Advanced Management—International (CAM-I), 1990, www.cam-i.org.

It is important to note the intersection of Activities in the CAM-I Cross. Both ABC and ABM focus improvements on activities. Activity improvements drive business improvements. Activity costs can be improved a variety of ways including:

- **Reducing the activities drivers (requests for work).** This can be done by working with cost objects (consumers) such as customers and product managers to reduce the number of work requests. This will be discussed briefly in the next section and in depth in Chapter 4.

- **Improving the quality of the work through the use of a variety of quality improvement techniques such as Total Quality Management (TQM) or Six Sigma.** During an ABC implementation, you and your team will identify non-value-added (NVA) activities. Even more frequently, you will uncover NVA tasks "marbled" in activities, similar to fat being marbled into good meat. Identification and prioritization techniques will be discussed in Chapters 3 and 4, respectively.

- **Increasing the throughput of the activities to decrease the unit cost of the activities.** Once improvements are made, either (a) process more work for the same cost, or (b) reduce resources and costs to reflect the lower effort required to complete the work.

- **Reducing the resource costs.** Most commonly, this involves better supplier sourcing and may include outsourcing and offshoring. Resource cost reductions will not be discussed in this book.

The largest opportunity to reduce product and customer costs resides in activity (process) improvement. Without improving activities, why would you expect reduced costs? As Albert Einstein stated, "Insanity is defined as doing the same thing over and over again and expecting different results."

Cost Object and Activity Driver Management

A lot of emphasis in cost and profitability improvement in ABC/M is appropriately placed on improving activities. However, many people overlook the importance of cost object and activity driver management. In my experience, cost object and activity driver management remain a relatively large untapped opportunity in ABC/M implementations.

To demonstrate the value of cost object management, let's start with a concept called Cliff Charts (or Whale Curves). Cliff Charts are used at many manufacturing and financial institutions to rank the profitability of products and customers. For a commercial banking line of business, Cliff Charts plot the most profitable to least profitable customers in order and look like Figure 1.7.

Figure 1.7 demonstrates that the approximately median customer is the "breakeven" customer with a maximum cumulative profit of $466 million; $190 million of value is destroyed by relationships with customers to the right of the midpoint. The company would be 69% more profitable without customers to the right of the midpoint. Of course, this simple improvement to the profitability assumes all costs are variable costs, which is not realistic. However, if the Cliff Chart were shown as marginal profit/loss only, you'd get roughly the same order of customers—the losers are still the losers.

How realistic is the slope of the curve? Royal Bank of Canada found that 17% of its customers accounted for 93% of the bank's profits, so it is not uncommon for the slope to be high in the beginning.[1]

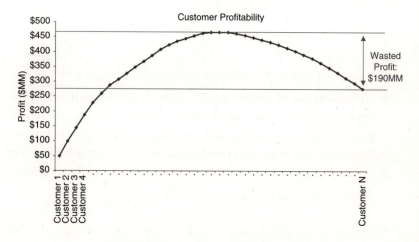

FIGURE 1.7   Customer Profitability Cliff Chart

Typical heights of the curve are 200–300% of the final customer (or product) profitability. In other words, the worst relationships destroy 100–200% of the corporate value.

The key is not to immediately exit those relationships, but to make them more profitable. Focus on the least profitable customers and migrate them to profitability through increased volume, share of wallet, behavior changes, price increases, and so on. If you are unable to move them into a profitable relationship, then exit them—our shareholders are better off without them. This will be covered in more detail in Chapter 4.

Cliff Charts can be used throughout the organization to rank profitability. Common Cliff Charts include:

- **Customer segment profitability within Retail and Individual lines.** Due to the large numbers of Retail and Individual customers, customers should be grouped to determine meaningful patterns and insights. For large, homogeneous customer bases like those in Retail and Individual lines, customer segment profitability (or profitability broken into deciles) is most appropriate.

- **Customer relationship profitability within Commercial and Institutional lines.** For smaller, highly variable customer bases like those with Commercial and Institutional lines, customer relationship profitability is most appropriate.

- **Branch profitability ranking within Retail lines.** While the composition of underlying products and customers clearly drives this ranking, branch profitability can be effectively used as a motivational tool. Additionally, investigate any differences in unused capacity to improve underutilized branches.

- **Relationship Manager profitability ranking within Commercial and Institutional lines.** Similarly, the composition of underlying products and customers drives this ranking, but the Cliff Chart can be an effective motivational tool for the sales force. Similarly, look to identify and improve ineffective sales personnel.

- **Product profitability within all lines.**

There are a few limitations of Cliff Charts to keep in mind. Cliff Charts do not usually contain the expected future profitability of the customer. Therefore, new customer relationships (less than six months) are often excluded from the analysis. Also, in the case of product Cliff Charts, they do not show product interdependence. However, even with its flaws, the Cliff Chart is a valuable and powerful tool for improving the corporate bottom line.

ABC without ABM

Over the years, I have heard no less than three consulting firms claim that they "invented" Activity-Based Costing. The date ranges were generally in the 1980s. One of the consultants had been around so long and claimed so many "inventions," we often joked that he probably invented farming, too. In the end, who cares who invented ABC? An ABC solution without implemented actions to improve the bottom line is worthless. I often ask my teams, "What is the value of better information?" The answer is: "Nothing . . . unless you use the information to drive results."

As a matter of fact, a great ABC implementation without ABM to improve the bottom line actually destroys shareholder value through the efforts and expenses required to implement ABC. One of the most common and damaging mistakes of ABC/M implementations is the overemphasis on ABC and the lack of emphasis on ABM. Never lose your focus on the end state. Drive improvements to the bottom line or the ABC/M implementation will be viewed (correctly) as a failure.

Remember to "begin with the end in mind." The remaining chapters in this book are written to help structure and implement ABC and ongoing ABM to drive results.

NOTE

1. Larry Selden and Geoffrey Colvin. *Killer Customers: Tell the Good from the Bad and Crush Your Competitors* (New York: Portfolio/Penguin, 2004).

CHAPTER **2**

Costing, Chargeback, and Pricing

There's no business like show business, but there are several businesses like accounting.

—David Letterman

DEFINE YOUR OBJECTIVES

Begin with the end in mind. The first step in implementing an ABC/ABM project is to determine the customers of the process and the final objectives of these customers. The SIPOC model is an excellent tool for determining how the customers' objectives will be fulfilled. SIPOC represents information and resource flow from suppliers to process inputs, converted in the process to output for the suppliers.

SIPOC: Suppliers → Input → Process → Output → Customers

To design the ABC/M system, start with the customers and work SIPOC right-to-left (COPIS). Who are the customers of your ABC system? You probably have three types of customers:

1. Lines of Business (LOBs) Consumers such as Product Managers, Market and Executive Management, and the LOB Chief Financial Officers (CFOs)
2. Shared Services Providers such as IT and HR
3. Cost Accounting Advisors, Implementers, Caretakers, Analysts

What are your customers' objectives? These objectives will drive the scope of your ABC model and become customer requirements.

Objectives (Use) of ABC/M

There are several common objectives that drive ABC/M implementations. All of these objectives have different design implications. Some of the most common objectives include:

- **Provide accurate product and customer costs based on true consumption of resources.** This is the primary reason for undertaking ABC. However, the value of this improved accuracy is zero unless it is used. Companies must utilize ABM to drive the value uncovered by ABC.

- **Improve the accuracy of cost assignments through chargeback.** This is the second most common use of ABC. Use ABC to develop a cost and rate for shared services to charge back to the LOBs. Once again, if this does not result in improvements to activities, product or customers, the value is zero.

- **Improve profitability analysis and strategic business planning.** Use ABC information to change the direction of the company by incorporating the information into the strategic business plan. This is much more of an ABM objective than ABC.

- **Focus on process improvement and cost reduction.** Coupling this type of ABM effort with Six Sigma or Total Quality Management (TQM) is often a good idea. ABC information feeds the Six Sigma Define, Measure, Analyze, Improve and Control (DMAIC) process and can be used to assist in the Control phase to monitor the process. Chapter 3 will highlight how ABC/M and Six Sigma connect through the use of Attributes.

- **Guide investment analysis and planning.** Similar to the support for strategic business planning, this ABM objective uses ABC to provide the direction of the company through both long- and short-term investing.

- **Provide internal baselines and internal/external benchmarks for comparison to identify improvement opportunities.** This is an ABM-driven improvement. Establish a baseline and improve against that baseline. Internally benchmark the company across regions or LOBs and improve the overall performance of the company. See Chapter 4 for a brief overview of the differences between baselines, benchmarks, and best practices.

- **Integrate operational control with performance measurement systems.** Use ABC/M to reinforce control and accountability throughout the organization. This is an effective way to get people to pay attention to the ABC results and drive improvements. If someone's bonus is attached to the use of ABC and the improvement to the P&L, it will happen.

Scope

- **Which areas will be incorporated into ABC/M? Front office and shared services? . . . or just shared services?** In order to get a full picture of product and customer profitability, the entire Build of Activities needs to be included: shared services *and* front office. If ABC/M will be used solely for process improvement, the scope can be much less ambitious—front office *or* shared services.

    During an ABC implementation, a line (front office) finance manager who professed to "really want to know" the cost of her products was initially surprised when I told her that we need to find out how the sales force is spending their time. "Why?" she asked, "Isn't ABC all about the back office costs?" The sales force was responsible for approximately 80% of most product costs in this LOB. We went on to discover a poor sales force process, poor sales metrics, and a misaligned incentive plan which rewarded the sales force exclusively on revenue without cross-sales, while the corporate strategy was based on improved profitability through cross-selling. Hmm . . . ABC is not all about the back office, is it?

■ **What are the cost objects? Products? Customers? LOBs?** Ideally, the ABC/M implementation is focused on products and customers. Be careful with a focus on LOBs or regions. Most of the time, while executive management may be compensated on LOB or regional performance, the distinction is fairly artificial. The profitability of the Colorado region of the Wholesale Banking LOB cannot be discussed without an understanding of the composition of the products and customers that make up this region/LOB combination. Since you do not plan to sell a "Colorado region of the Wholesale Bank," the profitability of the entity is irrelevant. What if one of the most profitable customers moves to another region? What if the regional map is redrawn? The regional manager should not get "high fives" or a lashing either way. Focus on customer and product profitability at all times. The by-products of regional and LOB profitability will follow.

If you are unable to determine a cost object list, the ABC/M implementation is off to a bad start. Early on in one ABC/M implementation, it became apparent that two LOBS did not clearly define products. Using a less accurate costing method, Corporate Accounting had been producing product costs for years for products that were not recognized by the product managers. Additionally, and more frightening, the product managers did not have a clear and meaningful definition of "product." Some product managers included a geographic dimension to product, as if the customers cared that the remittance processing was handled in Boulder, Colorado versus Chicago, Illinois. They had trouble distinguishing between product features and products. A clear way to determine what level to drive costs: Is there a Profit and Loss (P&L) and is someone accountable (is their compensation impacted) by changes to this P&L? Also, from a customer's perspective, what are they buying? That is a product. Think about it in terms of retail car sales. Customers buy a particular model which is the product. Stereo systems and floor mats are accessories, not products.

Frequency

■ **Is ABC/M a one-time event (a cost improvement study)? Or are the ABC/M results refreshed annually, quarterly, or monthly?** In my experience, ABC works best as a monthly reporting tool and ABM initiatives can be identified, driven, and reviewed quarterly or annually. Why? As you'll see, the source data for the resource cost pools is the general ledger (GL). It makes sense to synchronize the ABC results to the monthly GL reports. Using standard extract, transform and load (ETL) tools, ABC no longer needs to lag monthly GL reports. Additionally, since there can be large monthly cost variances on the GL due to the invoicing of large-ticket items, such as technology, a single month can be a poor yardstick with which to measure product or customer profitability.

■ **Will drivers be updated with the same frequency as the costs?** The typical initial answer to this is, "Please update all of the resource and activity drivers monthly." Ouch. In many cases, it is still not feasible to update resource and activity drivers on a monthly basis. For example, while some areas of an organization may track hours by activity and cost object, most areas do not have this level of sophistication. Many IT areas utilize labor tracking software to identify activities and cost objects. Most other areas do not. Therefore, update automated drivers monthly. All other drivers can be updated quarterly.

Reporting

■ **Is it "push" or "pull"?** Push reporting generally refers to a centrally-created, static, standard reporting package. Imagine a 100-page binder holding the standard reports, regardless if the binder is physical or virtual (online). Hopefully, the answers to all of your questions are somewhere in the binder. If not, the binder needs to expand next month. Standard television is an example of a push medium. Watch what is programmed or turn off the television.

Pull reporting generally refers to online, distributed, dynamic reporting. The Internet is an example of a pull medium. Find what you want when you want it. For ABC/M, online analytical processing (OLAP) tools are best for pull reporting. It is a good idea to have two sets of reporting tools: a standard set for monthly reporting with limited investigation and drill-in capabilities and a "power user" set to allow more free-form analysis. For example, Hyperion Reports fulfills the first need and Hyperion Analyzer fulfills the second.

■ **How is ABC progress reported? What will you track? What is actionable?** When ABC is just underway and just rolling out, much of the reporting will be informational—this is what we implemented . . . and here are the results. While this is appropriate in the rollout and education, when ABC/M becomes imbedded in your organization, try to limit your informational reporting to 20% and your actionable reporting to 80%. Report the negative outlier activities, products, and customers. Report on the action plans to improve the Net Income Before Taxes (NBIT). Report on the bottom line results of your ABC/M efforts as seen in Figure 2.1.

Figure 2.1 shows the original project target as a $20 million NIBT improvement by the end of 2009. The target was revised to reflect a $40 million NIBT improvement by the end of 2009. The validated sign-offs (validated by the LOB CFOs via a sign-off process) was just under $20 million in February 2008. The sign-off process is a confirmation of the documented and expected ABM initiative results. No NIBT benefits should be included in the overall ABM benefits without the physical sign-off of the financial organization. Their independence is an impartial attestation of the ABM benefits. The sign-off is a confirmation that the ABM benefits are included in the forecast and budget.

Now let's return to the SIPOC flow introduced in the beginning of this chapter. After gathering Customer objectives and requirements,

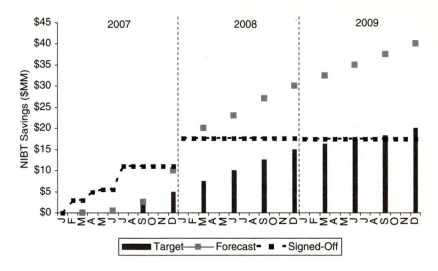

FIGURE 2.1 Tracking ABC/M Value

determine the Output required to meet these objectives within the confines of ABC. Required Output will drive the Process and ABC model design necessary to create the Output. The Process will drive Input requirements (activities and drivers) and the Input will define the Input Suppliers. The Suppliers are the ABC driver sources.

COSTING: ABSORPTION CHOICES

As mentioned earlier, the primary reason for undertaking an ABC implementation is to provide accurate product and customer costs based on true consumption of resources. To start the ABC design in the right direction, you'll have to address two common design choices: the choice between marginal and full absorption costing, and the choice among waterfall, reciprocal, and recursive costing.

There are generally two deeply divided camps regarding the subject of costing. Margin costing is generally favored by product managers and sales personnel. Full absorption costing is generally favored by Operations, Finance, and Accounting personnel. The camps remain deeply divided because each method is applicable in certain situations, but not in others.

Marginal Costing

Marginal Costing identifies the incremental cost of adding volume—it excludes the fixed costs of production—and is very useful for analyzing most sales decisions (i.e., transactions). For example, one minute before takeoff, an airline should sell any seat on the plane at a profit margin above the cost of the in-flight meal and the incremental fuel required for the additional weight of the passenger, luggage, and meal (assuming all other costs are fixed).

Margin Costing is closely related to the concept of costing for practical capacity. Practical capacity is equal to the total capacity less planned idle and excess capacity for protective purposes such as demand surges. Similarly, this concept is useful for analyzing sales and planning decisions. For example, if the electronic documentation process is running at 50% practical capacity and is planned to increase volume to 90% practical capacity, related product profitability, and sales incentives should be based on the 90% practical capacity analysis. Keep in mind, that costing for practical capacity is only realistic when the company is capable of balancing the workload (i.e., customers do not drive the workload timing). An example of an unbalanced workload in banking is activities associated with the ATM. Clearly, most customers use the ATMs between the hours of 8 AM and midnight. Incentives will not shift much ATM usage to 3 AM.

Even though "cost plus" pricing is not optimal (discussed later in this chapter), some product managers use the marginal cost to set a marginal price. Let's examine an example of the dangers of "cost plus" marginal pricing shown in Figure 2.2.

In Figure 2.2, the scanning process requires a piece of scanning equipment purchased for $200,000, depreciating over 10 years ($20,000/year) that scans 100,000 documents per year. For each new customer, you'll need to add $1,000 in variable cost (personnel). Each customer needs 10,000 documents scanned per year. For this example, let's assume that the expected usage of the scanning equipment is its practical capacity. What happens when the service is priced on the variable cost with a 50% markup?

The variable cost per scan is $1,000/10,000 or $0.10/scan. The price per scan with 50% markup is $0.15/scan. The fixed cost per scan

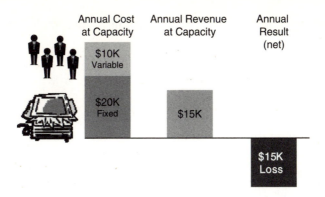

FIGURE 2.2 Marginal Pricing Example

at capacity is $20,000/100,000 or $0.20/scan. So, at capacity, the full revenue is $15,000 and the full cost is $30,000, resulting in a $15,000 loss for the shareholder. What happened? The marginal cost plus pricing did not have a large enough margin to cover the fixed costs. The breakeven price in this example was $0.30/scan.

In this example, "steady state" was assumed to be the practical capacity, but realistically, the steady state *maximum* is the practical capacity. To understand the anticipated costs per scan at the steady state, the company would have to estimate the number of scans sold (this should have been done in the scanning business case and the budget). If the steady state was only 50% of the practical capacity, the fixed costs would be $0.40/scan and the breakeven price would be $0.50/scan.

While caution should be used with marginal costing, it does have merits in special circumstances:

- Marginal analysis is useful for product entries and exits.
- Marginal analysis is useful for sales incentives and planning.
- Marginal analysis can be used to fill unused capacity, but this is also very complex and should be undertaken on a case-by-case basis.

Marginal pricing can be used to offset fixed costs on an exception basis (as shown in the airline example). However, if the exception becomes the rule and the product becomes unprofitable, the shareholder loses.

A special note of caution: Some employees may argue the fixed costs are "sunk" (i.e., one-time event in the past), so why is the product "burdened" with these costs? In all likelihood, you may hear this comment from the sales force in a cost plus pricing environment. If the price is based on the market rather than the cost, the cost has no bearing on the price.

Product costs must incorporate fixed costs for three reasons. First, to provide value to the shareholder, any business case must provide a positive net present value (NPV). At time zero, these costs were not fixed, but instead were an investment choice. The product needs to provide an appropriate NPV since time zero. Second, most equipment, software and facilities fixed costs are the best indicator we have of future investment requirements (growth and replacement costs). In that sense, fixed costs are not really fixed. They are just a step-function of costs with more capacity and time between steps. Third, if no product costs include fixed costs, all products may appear to be profitable while the company is unprofitable.

Full Absorption Costing

The concept of full absorption costing is quite simple: All costs are attributable to servicing a product or customer. All general ledger costs must "find a home" in a product and customer. If a cost does not increase customer or product profitability, why does the company incur the cost? If the cost does not provide value to the shareholder, get rid of it! This holds true for the back office, the sales force, and the corporate jet.

Advantages of full absorption costing include:

- It accurately reflects full P&L—not a reflection of what we wished had happened or a subset of the expenses.
- Using full absorption costing across all cost object dimensions forces the product, customer, and LOB costs to be equal (tie out).

- As mentioned above, full absorption costing forces a tough look at the value provided by all costs. If a cost does not increase shareholder value, eliminate it.

- It forces a conversation (and hopefully, action!) regarding unprofitable products/customers due to underutilized capacity or wasteful overhead.

- Full absorption costing eliminates the possibility of having all "profitable" products and customers, yet having an unprofitable company. Marginal costing enables this concept.

However, there are also disadvantages of full absorption costing. The disadvantages are generally related to start-up and declining products. Disadvantages of full absorption costing include:

- New product/customer offerings requiring a large fixed cost investment may appear unprofitable.

- If full absorption costing is used to set a price, the price may be set too high for the market. The solution here is very simple: Do not use cost to set the market price!

- Exiting product/customer offerings may result in a temporary undue burden for the remaining products which may lead people to exit even more products/customers (the so-called Death Spiral described in Eli Goldratt's Theory of Constraints). For example, at one ABC implementation, the exit of the Auto Dealer business slightly reduced the profitability of the Recreational Finance business due to the increased fixed costs assigned to Recreational Finance. This could, in turn, cause the Recreational Finance business to appear to be unprofitable which may cause an exit of this business.

For mature products at or near capacity (steady state), full absorption costing is completely appropriate. For new product offerings, the ABC model can be adapted to show both the estimated cost at steady state and the full absorption cost including excess capacity.

Bottom line: Full absorption should be the primary costing method with visibility into marginal costs and unused capacity, as needed. The

ABC system should be based on full absorption costing, but contain marginal costing information (Fixed/Variable attributes, discussed in Chapter 3). Additionally, the ABC system should be capable of modeling unused capacity in appropriate areas.

COSTING: DRIVING COSTS FROM SUPPORT AREAS

The other large design choice faced in an ABC implementation is the choice among waterfall, reciprocal, and recursive costing. All are methods to drive costs from the cost centers incurring the costs to cost objects responsible for the costs. We'll start with the simplest method first: waterfall costing.

Waterfall Costing

Let's take two large, common, shared services cost centers in financial services: HR and IT. HR provides recruiting, benefits, planning, and displacement services for the entire corporation, including IT. IT is a customer of HR and generally receives a direct charge to the IT cost centers. Prior to ABC, HR costs are often based on the headcount of the serviced area. Similarly, IT provides the technology infrastructure, support, and project development services for the entire corporation, including HR. As such, HR is a customer of IT and also, generally receives a direct charge to the HR costs centers.

So, what do you do? Well, one method is waterfall costing, shown in Figure 2.3.

The concept is quite simple. Some functional area (usually HR or IT), sits on "top" of the waterfall. In Figure 2.3, HR can assign costs directly to all cost centers or activities of other functions. HR assigns $100 to IT, $300 to Operations, and $1,600 to the Front Office, based on activity drivers for the variety of activities performed by HR. Notice this is not a "peanut butter" allocation of pre-ABC costs based on a single driver (headcount).

The next step in the waterfall costing approach is to assign all of the IT costs (including the $100 assigned from HR) to the remaining "downstream" functions, based on ABC. So, IT assigns $7,100 to

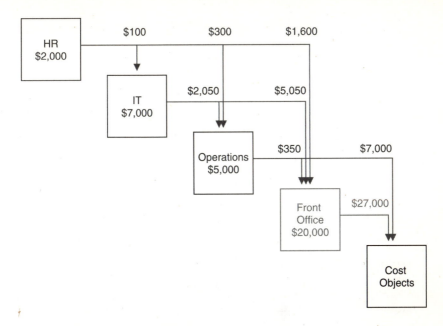

FIGURE 2.3 Waterfall Costing

Operations ($2,050) and the Front Office ($5,050). The waterfall continues until all of the costs are driven to the final cost objects from the activities required by these products and customers.

While this method is the least accurate of the three discussed here, it is still much better than non-ABC. This is the type of ABC system I implemented more than ten years ago, primarily due to the past limitations of financial and ABC software systems. Waterfall costing is easy to understand and explain. While the method is quick and accurate, it is not as accurate as the following two methods.

Reciprocal Costing

Reciprocal costing improves the accuracy over waterfall costing. It is used in shared services organizations to provide a one-time assignment (via ABC) between the shared services organizations before assigning the costs to the Front Office and Cost Objects. A high-level example of reciprocal costing is shown in Figure 2.4.

In Step 1 of the above example, HR assigns $400 using ABC to IT ($100) and Operations ($300), leaving $1,600 unassigned. IT assigns

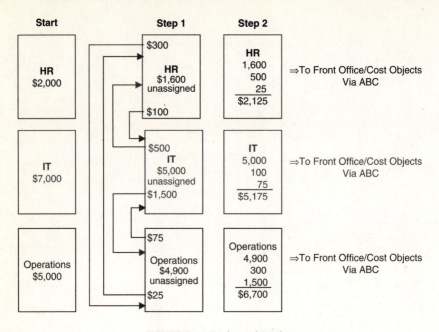

FIGURE 2.4 Reciprocal Costing

$2,000 using ABC to HR ($500) and Operations ($1,500), leaving $5,000 unassigned. Similarly, Operations assigns $100 using ABC to HR ($75) and IT ($25), leaving $4,900 unassigned.

In Step 2, using ABC, each of the shared services assigns the "new" total to the Front Office or directly to cost objects. For example, Operations originally had $5,000 to assign, but based on usage of HR and IT resources, Operations needs to assign $6,700 via its activities to the Front Office and cost objects.

Recursive Costing

With the advent of more powerful ABC tools, it has been possible for several years to implement recursive costing. This method involves creating the ABC model without regard to waterfall or reciprocal costing. The model iteratively assigns costs between functions until a user-defined low threshold is reached.

For example, in the reciprocal example shown in Figure 2.4, recursive costing would take the newly assigned $525 in Step 3 of HR and assign it to IT (5% or $26.25), Ops (15% or $78.75) and Front Office or directly to cost objects (80% or $420). Similarly, this iterative assignment would occur for both IT and Operations until the user-defined threshold of materiality was met and practically all costs were assigned to Front Office or cost objects.

In my view, while it is certainly mathematically and technically possible to implement recursive costing, the complexity involved in explaining and tracing recursive costing is not worth the improvement in accuracy. In most cases, reciprocal costing provides the best mix of understandability, tracing (accountability), and accuracy.

CHARGEBACK

Early on, it was common for companies implementing ABC to have stand-alone reporting for ABC results. These reports became the basis of ABM improvements. These reports did not necessarily "tie" to other management reporting. Since the focus was on improving the bottom line quickly, rather than integrating ABC, people temporarily looked past the disconnect.

As ABC matured, corporations drove for "one version of the truth." This meant using ABC as the basis of the chargeback system to provide one picture of the product and customer costs. ABC became a module or plug-in for corporate Enterprise Resource Planning (ERP) systems.

Management Reporting

In today's environment, it is essential for ABC results to feed management reporting. If you want to get Product Management's attention regarding product profitability, use ABC on the management P&L. Management reporting should be clean and crisp for all products and customer segments (cost objects) with the ability to drill down to more detail.

For the standard set of monthly reports, both P&L and graphics-dominated reports (drill-downs with pie charts and trending reports) are useful. After the roll-out of ABC, when the organization has a good handle on the methodology and flow behind the ABC data, migrate to exception reporting. Which activities are the highest priorities

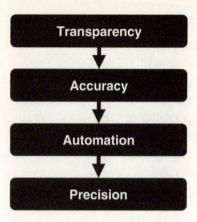

FIGURE 2.5 ABC Management Reporting Priorities

for improvement? Which products' and customers' profits need to be improved the most?

It is important to prioritize needs within management reporting. My standard philosophy in ABC reporting is shown in Figure 2.5.

Transparency

Transparency enables a common understanding throughout the organization. Transparency is needed to "stop the bleeding" and to enable CFOs and product managers help improve costing accuracy. Rather than having several cost accountants and ABC implementers pouring through the ABC data to find improvements, pilot the results using great transparent reporting to all of the CFOs and product managers impacted by the ABC implementation. You will find and improve the overall system much faster.

The lack of transparency covers up many evils of costing systems. During the project initiation and early data gathering of one ABC/M implementation, the costing area assured my team that they already had implemented ABC. Of course, I asked to see the details from a user perspective. Costs were provided to users in three activity roll-ups called Sales & Acquisition, Maintenance, and Transaction with no drill-down capability (i.e., transparency). At best, the Corporate Business Checking (DDA) product manager could see the information shown in Figure 2.6 on a monthly basis.

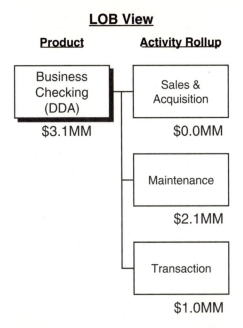

LOB View

Product   **Activity Rollup**

Business Checking (DDA)
$3.1MM

Sales & Acquisition
$0.0MM

Maintenance
$2.1MM

Transaction
$1.0MM

FIGURE 2.6 Non-Transparent LOB View Checking

What actionable information could the product manager glean from Figure 2.6? Nothing. There was no drill-down and no attributes. What is behind the $2.1 million in Maintenance? Apparently, the product sold itself (and set itself up!) since there were no meaningful sales or setup costs associated with this product. Strange . . .

Well, surely we can clear this up within the cost accounting system, right? The drill-down in the cost accounting system which was not available to users is shown in Figure 2.7.

Here it becomes more perplexing. Both Sales & Acquisition and Maintenance continued to be vague with only a single "detailed" activity rolling up to each. The allocation (not assignment) logic for the Transaction activities was not available without a system deep-dive and most disturbing was the fact that many "support" activities were actually allocated (not assigned) outside the costing system. Literally, one person in the back office was allocating costs with an offline spreadsheet and feeding the costing system. Was it any wonder that the product managers were frustrated, confused, and found the costing data to be unusable?

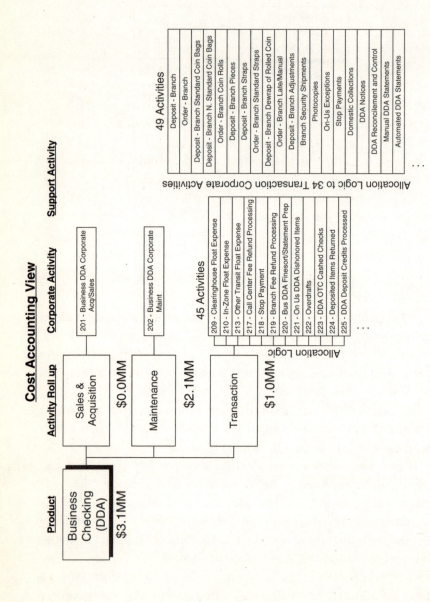

FIGURE 2.7 Non-Transparent Costing Accounting View

30

Transparency was the first step in bringing the product managers on board. Transparency enabled the next step: accuracy.

Accuracy

Both cost and volume accuracy must be improved to make better activity, product, customer, and channel decisions. Some people may question why accuracy follows transparency. Doesn't ABC information have to be accurate? Of course ABC information needs to be accurate, but having transparent information and reporting improves ABC's accuracy and is the highest priority.

Returning to the example above, we uncovered the information shown in Figure 2.8 after transparency was complete.

It was clear that several steps needed to be undertaken to improve the accuracy of the existing system. For example, 68% of the product costs were Maintenance and virtually no costs were attributable to sales, acquisition, and set up activities. Business Checking appeared to sell itself (and set itself up on the system!). Additionally, in Figure 2.8, it is clear that several other products such as ACH and Wires were "parking" costs in Business Checking. Unfortunately, it is not uncommon for non-ABC systems to allocate costs from a marginally profitable product to a highly profitable product, thereby distorting the true product costs for both products. The marginally profitable product looks more profitable than it really is, while the highly profitable product appears less profitable than it is.

Lastly, there was an accuracy issue with something that is not observed in Figure 2.8. However, since the costs were allocated outside of the costing system, the impact and method were undiscovered by the users. In this case, support costs were incorrectly assigned to corporate activities. An offline spreadsheet allocated the cost of coin replenishment to ATM withdrawals. Unfortunately, the bank had no coin capability at any of its ATMs. Without transparency, it required the team to perform a lot of forensic accounting work to unravel this inaccuracy.

Automation

Most ABC implementations are somewhat over-engineered initially and are scaled back after the first iteration. As you solidify the ABC

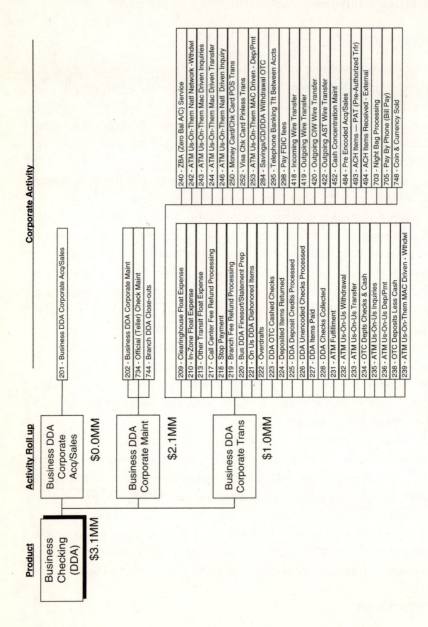

FIGURE 2.8 Lack of Costing Accuracy Example

32

system through transparency and improved accuracy, automate the driver collection. Automation of drivers (both activity and resource) is essential to maintaining a costing system and having a stable, repeatable process. One of the key tools to enabling this automation is the Extract, Transform, and Load (ETL) tool.

Additionally, pay particular attention to existing automated data sources and your ability to use those sources for the ABC/M system. In particular, the IT billing system probably contains information by activity (the IT system development life cycle), the branch staffing model may contain the time and motion studies required for the ABC system, and the sales module of the CRM system, such as Siebel, may contain information regarding the time and effort required to sell different products.

Precision

Least important during implementation is precision. Whether or not we are confident in the product cost to the fourth decimal place comes later. Let's start with the first two digits!

As indicated by the emphasis on transparency in Figure 2.5, it is important to allow "power users" the ability to drill down to investigate charges. However, to avoid unproductive, interdepartmental conflicts, it is best to stop transparency at the activity level for shared services chargeback. Further transparency to the resource level may give the false impression that the LOBs can determine project and operations staffing. If an LOB truly needs to dictate the resources to be used on particular projects or processes, the shared service organization is not doing its job. Staffing (and other resourcing) is part of the shared service organization control and is part of fulfilling a work request. For example, if an LOB solution requires in-house technology development, the application development area is responsible for determining the appropriate staffing (business analysts, database administrators, junior programmers, senior programmers, testers) to meet the business needs. The LOB should focus on the quality, cost, and timing of the project.

Goals and Activity-Based Budgeting

Since ABC/M identifies many different ways to improve the bottom line, there are many opportunities for goal setting, including the reflection of these goals in the budget. At a high level, it is not un-common to achieve a 5–10% improvement in profitability as a result of the implementation of ABC/M. Product managers and line CFOs should incorporate improvement identification and, more importantly, bottom line results into their goals.

While this book does not address Activity-Based Budgeting (ABB) in detail, it is the third pillar of a fully implemented ABC/M methodology. On its surface, ABB is very simple: Product and customer volumes drive the budget. The number of new accounts drives the Open New Account activity which, in turn, demands a number of resources be assigned to Open New Account. While it is a common-sense extension of ABC/M, Will Rogers did say, "There is nothing as uncommon as common sense."

During one implementation of ABC/M, I discovered that the shared services division (Operations and IT historically presented its budget before the LOBs provided their volume forecasts for the upcoming year. Talk about the tail wagging the dog! There was no accountability by the LOBs for achieving their volume projections. The shared services area made its own projections on volumes without in-depth conversations with the lines and ended up in a no-win situation year after year. Why were the shared services costs so high? Well, shared services did not expect those volumes. The LOBs expected these volumes, so why didn't shared services expect these volumes? Or, if the LOB actual volumes are lower than the LOB budgeted volumes, why can't shared services cut costs? Well, shared services budgeted these lower volumes and budgeted the reduced service requirements. Both series of questions demonstrate the lack of accountability and control when the budget is not based on a set of common volumes owned by the LOBs, but developed with input from shared services.

RATES

As part of implementing any chargeback methodology you will have to determine, communicate, and, unfortunately, sometimes defend the rate philosophy. Rates come in three basic types: actual, standard, and expected.

Actual Rates

Actual rates are the most straightforward to handle in the ABC/M system. Start with the actual general ledger and, as much as possible, use actual monthly drivers to create actual rates and chargebacks. Since every dollar flows to the cost objects, there are no residual costs.

Sounds great, right? Well, not so fast . . .

The issue encountered with actual rates is that they fluctuate month to month. For example, invoices tend to be "chunky" with large invoices wreaking havoc with the rates. Even more common is the variance in product volumes with a relatively fixed cost structure. The company cannot efficiently adjust capacity on a monthly basis to accommodate large, unsustained product volume variances.

The issue with actual rates is that you may spend more time explaining the monthly rate variances than improving the bottom line.

Standard Rates

Standard rates are most appropriately used for activities dominated by dedicated resources with a practical capacity as shown in Figure 2.9. The practical capacity is the measured standard capacity less the time for expected and unexpected maintenance. The left side of Figure 2.9 depicts the information required to develop standard and expected rates. The right side of Figure 2.9 provides the actual performance of the activity.

Budget

Print Forms

Printer A   Printer B

Budget Expense:	$100/month
Budget Volume:	15,000 pages/month
Capacity:	20,000 pages/month

Actual

Print Forms

Printer A   Printer B

Actual Expense:	$110
Actual Volume:	17,500 pages

FIGURE 2.9 Standard Rate Example

The standard rate for the Print Form activity is $0.005/page ($100/20,000 pages). The expected rate will be $0.0067/page ($100/15,000 pages). Figure 2.10 summarizes the results of the different rate types.

Notice the simplicity of the actual rate. There is never any residual, but the rate will change monthly. Conversely, the standard and expected rates do not change monthly, but there is a residual. Additionally, in the standard rate line there is a determination of the cost of excess capacity. As explained in the marginal pricing discussion, this excess capacity is useful for case-by-case marginal pricing decisions. Standard rates and excess capacity identification go hand-in-hand and should be used only for activities with a rated practical capacity.

It is possible and appropriate to use standard times created by time and motion studies to determine excess capacity of front office (branch) operations. After the time and motion studies are complete, the resources are assigned to activities based on standard time multiplied by the activity volumes. The remaining available time is then assigned to Wait for Customer or Idle Time which is, in essence, excess capacity. This time and motion information is used for both ABC calculations and staffing decisions.

However, without time and motion studies, it is impractical to use standard costs for multifunction resources. For example, in IT is there a rated practical capacity for the time it takes a database administrator to design a database for a new system? Not really. The closest measurement of this type of productivity is something called function points (which is the topic of several books and requires extensive training to accurately estimate). The less operational, more complex, more time-of-day dependent and more ambiguous the activity, the less appropriate standard rates become.

An added complexity of standard rates is the accountability of the excess capacity. If excess capacity were driven to products based on the actual volume, a product manager would have incentive to overestimate the volumes and avoid being penalized (from a cost perspective) for not meeting those volumes. Similarly, a product manager should not be discouraged from using excess capacity. In Figure 2.8, three product managers (Product A, Product B, Product C) budget monthly

	Budget Volume	Actual Volume	Budget $	Charge	Excess Capacity	Residual	Actual $
Standard Rate = $0.005/page	15,000	17,500	$100	$87.50 (17,500 × $.005)	$12.50 (20,000 – 17,500) × $.005	$10 ($110 – $100)	$110
Expected Rate = $0.0067/page	15,000	17,500	$100	$117.25 (17,500 × $.0067)	N/A	–$7.25 ($110 – $117.25)	$110
Actual Rate = Varies Monthly	15,000	17,500	$100	$110	N/A	N/A	$110

FIGURE 2.10 Comparison of Rate Types for Print Forms

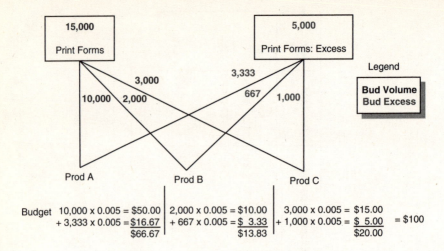

FIGURE 2.11 Standard Rate and Excess Capacity Budget

volumes of 10,000 items, 2,000 items and 3,000 items, respectively. This causes Operations to purchase a printer with a rated practical capacity of 20,000 items per month.

In Figure 2.11, the excess capacity costs are assigned to the products based on the proportion of the budgeted volumes. Now, let's assume actual forms printed were 12,500 (Product A), 2,000 (Product B), and 3,000 (Product C). If the excess capacity—now only 2,500—were assigned based on the proportion of the actual volumes, Product A would be penalized for using some of the excess capacity since a high proportion of the excess costs would go to Product A.

A better theoretical alternative is to assign the excess capacity based on the budgeted volumes as shown in Figure 2.12.

While Product A's actual costs have increased as a result of more volume, the excess capacity assigned to Product A is only $8.33 which is less than the $8.93 that would have been assigned if the assignment had been based on the proportion of actual volume. Also, notice how Product B and Product C have benefitted by Product A's use of the excess capacity.

Intuitively, the excess capacity needs to be driven on the budgeted volumes since most capital purchases are based on the budget, not the actuals. Operations cannot wait for the volume to arrive before

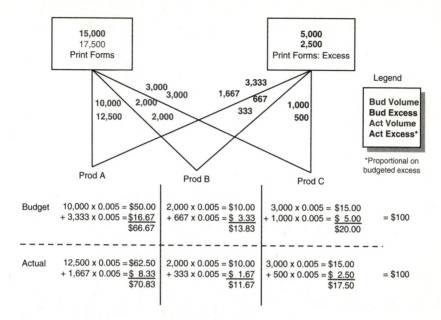

FIGURE 2.12 Excess Capacity Assigned Proportional to Budget

purchasing the equipment, so the driving force behind the purchase is the budget, not the actual volumes.

Personally, I have never implemented a chargeback with excess capacity assigned in this manner. The complexities are beyond the stage of any of my ABC/M implementations or post-implementations. However, I did spend considerable effort determining the fairest approach to standard costing and the issue of excess capacity.

Expected Rates

Expected rates are the most common rates used in ABC/M. As seen in Figure 2.10, expected rates are simply the budgeted costs divided by the budgeted volumes. Expected rates are best when the standard rates are unknown or undeterminable, as shown in Figure 2.13.

What is the capacity of the resources (programmers) used in the Design Program activity? How fast do they design (think)? It is truly unanswerable and will vary from program to program, programmer to programmer, and day today. It is much more appropriate to use an

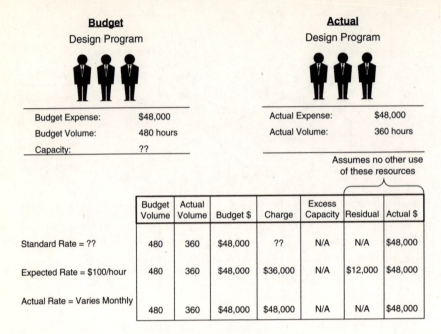

FIGURE 2.13 Expected Rate Example

expected rate for this type of activity. Note the lack of realism shown in Figure 2.13. The expected rate has a residual of $12,000 and assumes that these resources cannot be used for other activities (such as Code Program). In reality, these resources are multi-use and will be redeployed to work on other activities rather than sit idle. This reinforces the fact that expected rates are most appropriate for this type of activity, since people are the ultimate multifunctional resource. There should be no "Wait for Work" for salaried programmers. Programmers' activities are not driven by a daily or hourly metric such as the number of customers and customer wait times.

Typically staffing models differ greatly between branch staffing and IT staffing models. Branch staffing models are generally set to achieve customer service levels during peak hours without more than 30% excess capacity. Conversely, IT staffing models typically staff full-time employees near the minimum required for the year (the valley) and augment the staff with contractors. This provides employment flexibility while minimizing costs.

BANK BRANCH PROFITABILITY

Within financial services, bank branch costing and profitability is somewhat unique. Deposit accounts provide an ongoing funding source (revenue). This revenue stream continues as long as the account is open. The account does not need to be active to provide revenue.

Additionally, active accounts drive expenses on a monthly basis: through deposits, withdrawals, payments, transfers, inquiries, and monthly maintenance (statements). Expenses are incurred across a variety of service channels including the branches.

Significant branch profitability inaccuracies occur when the branch receiving the revenue benefit is not the same branch incurring the expense of servicing the account. As you will see in the next section, due to the fluid nature of customer movements and behavior patterns, ABC/M models must match revenue and expenses by account to an owning branch to generate an accurate picture of branch profitability.

This potential revenue/expense mismatch does not occur in most retail businesses. If you purchase a shovel at the hardware store, all of the revenue associated with that transaction is recognized by the store at that time. The expenses, both direct and indirect, are also assigned to that store.

Owning versus Servicing Branches

Example 1: Same Owning and Servicing Branches

Imagine a simple branch network with three branches: X, Y, and Z. Three customers each open a deposit account at each of the branches (nine total accounts from nine customers), as shown in Figure 2.14. Branches X, Y, and Z each "own" three accounts. On a monthly basis, the branches' income statements will show interest income revenue for the three accounts. Since the customers only go to their owning branches for servicing, the branch profitability calculation is simple. The funding revenue is already matched to the servicing expense.

Example 2: Different Owning and Servicing Branches

However, in the real world, the owning and servicing branches are frequently different for each customer. Figure 2.15 shows a simplified

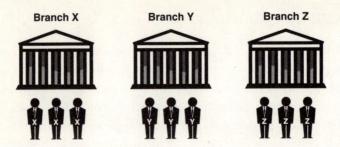

FIGURE 2.14 Owning Branches are the Servicing Branches

example. As in Figure 2.14, three customers each open a deposit account at each of the three branches (nine total accounts from nine customers). However, in Figure 2.15 two of the Branch Z customers perform their entire branch banking services in Branch Y.

What happened to branch profitability? Well, if no adjustments are made:

- Branch X profitability remained the same between Figures 2.14 and 2.15.
- Branch Y profitability decreased between the two figures due to the increased costs (increased staffing) associated with servicing the additional Branch Z customers.
- Branch Z profitability increase between the two figures due to reduced costs (reduced staffing) due to the drop in customers serviced.

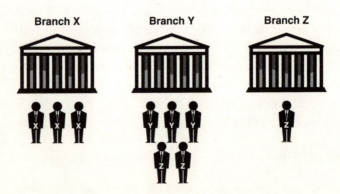

FIGURE 2.15 Different Owning and Servicing Branches

This situation is very inaccurate and misleading. Why should Branch Y be penalized for servicing Branch Z's customers? If someone blindly decided to close the least profitable branches, they would target Branch Y. What a mistake! If the branch customers base their primary bank on servicing, deposits from both Branch Y and Z would be driven off, while only saving the expenses associated with Branch Y.

In order to determine branch profitability accurately, the owning revenue and the servicing expense must be aligned. This is done through inter-branch charges and credit offsets. In Figure 2.15, variable expenses associated with servicing Branch Z customers are charged back to Branch Z. The offsetting credit associated with this charge is made to Branch Y to reduce its expense base. In this way, the branch profitability in Figure 2.15 is exactly equal to the branch profitability in Figure 2.14.

Re-Domiciling

Of course, there are many reasons why customers open an account at one branch and service the account from a second branch. The three most common reasons are:

- Change in work or home address
- Opened the account near work, but obtain services near home (or vice versa)
- A branch was added (or removed) from the network

These three reasons result in a lot of owning/servicing initial and ongoing discrepancies. Rather than letting these discrepancies continue to grow and degrade the performance of the ABC/M system, the organization needs to implement annual re-domiciling.

Re-domiciling involves transferring the account ownership from the current owning branch to the branch with the dominant number of servicing transactions. Figure 2.16 shows the impact of re-domiciling the customers in Figure 2.15.

Notice that the former Branch Z customers serviced by Branch Y are now considered Branch Y customers. The account ownership was

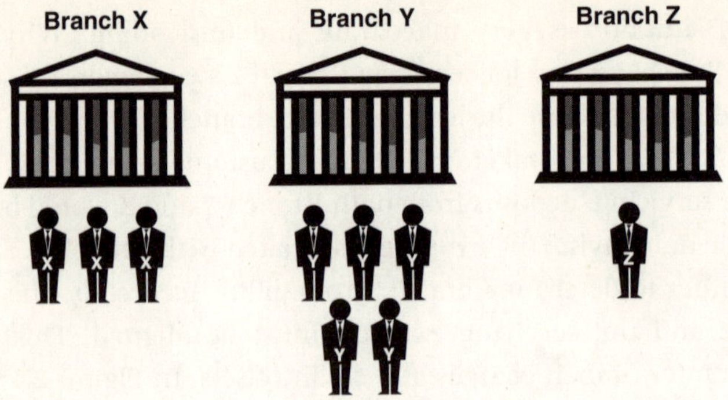

FIGURE 2.16 Re-Domiciling to align Owning and Servicing Branches

transferred from Branch Z to Branch Y. As a result of re-domiciling, fewer inter-branch charges and credit offsets will be required of the ABC/M system.

Other Credit Offsets

Outside of the bank branch network, there is little value in a cost center level credit offset, so implement the minimal acceptable level of credit offset. This minimal acceptable level is generally the highest practical consolidation point. Try not to allow credit offsets to occur lower than one level beneath an LOB or support area roll-up.

PRICING

Even within the financial community, it is common to hear people use two very different terms interchangeably: cost and price. Cost is the collective expense required to create and deliver the product. On the other hand, price is what is charged for the product—either in the market or within the company. Cost and price are related since they determine profitability. However, in order to maximize profit, price and cost should be independently determined. This section outlines several considerations required for effective pricing.

Consumption

At one client, the words "invoice" and "chargeback" were forbidden due to negative connotations. The ABC/M team was directed to use the term "Consumption Report" as we implemented ABC/M. In the end, I grew fond of the term. The term "Consumption Report" implies that the costs are not controlled by the internal or external customer— only the consumption of these costs is controllable.

My wife used to work for the world's largest food company, so I often use their candy bars to demonstrate the difference between cost and price, and between cost control and consumption control. The cost of cocoa and other food commodities changes on an hourly basis, but the price of the candy bar does not. As a consumer, my only choice is, "How many of those candy bars do I want to consume for the price?" The efficiency and quality of the candy bar production is determined by the company's management and, ultimately, the shareholders—not by the consumer.

Figure 2.17 depicts the relationship of support organizations (producers) and LOBs (consumers) within a corporation.

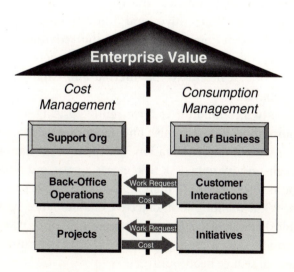

FIGURE 2.17 Cost and Consumption Control

Work requests are initiated by the LOBs on behalf of the customers through customer interactions or initiatives. It is these work requests (drivers) that cause support areas to use resources to complete the work requests. The use of these resources results in costs that are then assigned to the LOBs (chargeback), products and customers.

Support organizations own the cost and are focused on efficiency. This encompasses an emphasis on meeting the LOBs and customer requirements (including high quality) for the best possible long-term cost.

LOBs own the volumes and should focus on the drivers they can control or influence: activity drivers and customer behavior. The discussions between LOBs and support organizations are critical to overall expense management. Changes in volumes (work requests, above) result in increases or decreases to variable expenses in the support organizations. Large changes in volumes may even result in changes to fixed costs.

Incentive Pricing

An added level of sophistication and complexity of any chargeback system is introduced if incentive (and disincentive) pricing is added to the mix. ABC determines the costs of the activities for products and customers. However, there are times when the cost alone does not provide enough incentive for internal and external customers to change behavior.

There are two common uses for incentive pricing. One common use is a disincentive price to punish and discourage a certain behavior. During one ABC/M implementation, we discovered that one out of every six high-priority help desk tickets was a password reset. Several business units averaged more than 2.5 password reset calls annually per person. While the long-term objective of automating password resets was quickly established, a short-term punitive price was set at five times the cost to send a message to remember passwords and enable the help desk to reduce headcount.

Other common uses of a combination of incentive and disincentive pricing are migration from an old process to a new process, migration from an old technology standard to a new technology standard, and migration from a more popular time of day to a less popular time of day. This incentive/disincentive pricing has been around for decades in the IT world and was commonly used for peak versus off-peak pricing of mainframe time. Clearly, the actual cost of the mainframe remained relatively constant between 8 AM and 8 PM and from 8 PM to 8 AM with a slight decrease of energy costs from the utility companies (another form of incentive pricing). However, in order to avoid buying additional mainframes to cover the maximum first shift peak usage, customers were encouraged through incentive/ disincentive pricing to shift work to the off-peak hours from 8 PM to 8 AM.

Similarly, nonstandard items can be disincentive priced to discourage nonstandard purchases. For example, I have implemented disincentive pricing to discourage nonstandard computer monitors.

As with standard pricing, start with a 100% cost-based chargeback and then tweak the chargeback to modify behavior.

Volume and Cost Accountability

So, who is accountable for what? And why? Let's define accountability at each stage of the annual business life cycle: budget, actual results, forecast, and residuals.

- Budget Responsibilities
    Lines of Business
  - Plan monthly volumes per product. It is not realistic to expect that the LOBs can plan all support area volumes. At a minimum, the LOBs are expected to plan and commit to the number of new, outstanding and departed customers by product. In a homogeneous customer base, such as a consumer LOB, these volumes can be used to determine more granular product and customer volumes pertinent to the support organizations. In a diverse customer base, such as an institutional LOB, more information regarding the customer will be required to adequately prepare support organizations for the upcoming volume changes.

- Agree to service levels with the support organizations. Commitments to timeliness and quality also impact the resources required.

  Support Organizations

- Plan resources required (fixed and variable) to meet the LOBs volume projections and associated expenses.
- Agree to service levels with the LOBs. Commitments to timeliness and quality also impact the resources required.

■ Actual Results and Forecast Responsibilities

Lines of Business

- Deliver volumes per product in the budgeted months.
- Maintain rolling 12- to 18-month volume forecasts. At a minimum, the LOBs are expected to forecast the number of new, outstanding and departed customers by product, similar to the LOB budget responsibilities.

  Support Organizations

- Adjust variable resources to meet LOB volumes.
- If possible, adjust fixed resources to meet LOB volumes. It is understood that fixed costs, by their very definition, are difficult to mitigate in a short period of time. However, the support area should still make the effort to adjust fixed costs.
- Forecast expenses based on future resource levels. Of course, these future resource levels are based on the LOB forecast.

■ Residuals Responsibilities

Lines of Business

- Held accountable for any volume variances.
- Held accountable for any changes to the **fixed** portion of the unit costs × (planned volume – actual volume). Since the fixed portion of the unit costs is driven by the LOBs, it is only appropriate to hold the LOBs accountable for the residuals.

  Support Organizations

- Held accountable for any changes to the **variable** portion of the unit costs × (planned volume – actual volume). Since the variable portion of the unit costs is driven by the support organizations, it is only appropriate to hold these areas accountable for the residuals.

Residuals

In any chargeback situation using a standard or expected rate, there will be an over- or under-recovery and an associated residual cost or credit. The residuals can be a result of variance in budgeted volumes, costs, or both. Any significant residual should be resolved quarterly to get a more accurate picture of product profitability. In the past, I have used a threshold of 5% for the definition of "significant" residuals for each product.

Additionally, if the rates used are expected to continue to build residuals, update the rates rather than wait for the quarterly adjustments. Use the LOB volume and forecast and support area cost forecast to make that determination. A linear regression of the year-to-date (YTD) actual results will provide a sanity check on the forecast. The next section describes the analysis required to determine if a residual is appropriate. Similar to residual recovery, allow rate changes no more frequently than once per quarter.

Let's walk through an example of the accountability level described above using residuals. Figure 2.18 demonstrates the final result of the budget process. The LOB and the support area agreed to a budget based on volumes driven by internal and external factors.

Monthly, the "rate times volume" (R × V) chargeback is compared to the actual costs and volumes. At the end of the quarter, the residuals are moved to the appropriate products.

Who is accountable for the residuals? Figure 2.19 depicts accountability of an under-recovery. As stated above, the LOB is accountable for the volume variance and the support area is accountable for the cost variances unrelated to the volume variances.

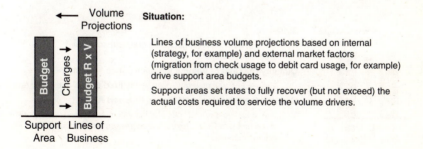

Situation:

Lines of business volume projections based on internal (strategy, for example) and external market factors (migration from check usage to debit card usage, for example) drive support area budgets.

Support areas set rates to fully recover (but not exceed) the actual costs required to service the volume drivers.

FIGURE 2.18 Annual ABB Budget Results

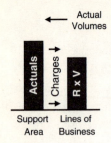

Situation:

Lines of business chargeback is less than support area actual results.

Quantify the Cost of Volume Variance (Lines of Business):

The volume variance multiplied by the fixed portion of the unit rate.

Quantify the Cost Control Variance (Support Area):

The actual volume multiplied by the variance of the variable portion of the unit rate PLUS: Fixed cost increases not associated with volume increases.

FIGURE 2.19 Under-Recovery Accountability

Figure 2.20 depicts accountability of an over-recovery. Once again, the LOB is accountable for the volume variance and the support area is accountable for the cost variances unrelated to the volume variances.

The consistency of accountability is straightforward and needs to be incorporated into monthly tracking and quarterly action. As a target for rate changes, my implementation and ongoing ABC/M teams determined that less than 25% of the rates should change on an annual basis. This is indicative of an adequate budgeting process. A stretch goal of changing 10% (or less) of the rates indicated an excellent budgeting process (i.e., high predictability and achievement).

Residual Determination: Avoiding Overcorrection

Frequently, inexperienced chargeback teams make residual distributions and rate adjustments when the adjustments are not warranted. In these cases, of course, the same time will have to reverse the

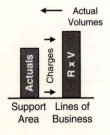

Situation:

Lines of business chargeback is greater than support area actual results.

Quantify the Cost of Volume Variance (Lines of Business):

The volume variance multiplied by the fixed portion of the unit rate.

Quantify the Cost Control Variance (Support Area):

The actual volume multiplied by the variance of the variable portion of the unit rate PLUS: Fixed cost increases not associated with volume increases.

FIGURE 2.20 Over-Recovery Accountability

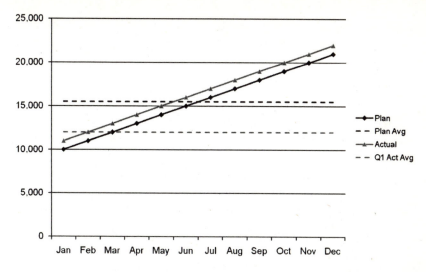

FIGURE 2.21 Plan vs. Actual Volumes—The Residual Problem

residual adjustments and possibly the rate changes later in the year. Why does this happen and how can it be avoided?

A simplified example of the underlying problem is shown in Figure 2.21.

For the purposes of this example, let's assume the volumes represent sales figures, so that a positive between actual and plan is a good thing. In Figure 2.21, notice the planned volumes increase from 10,000 in January to 21,000 in December, resulting in a monthly average of 15,500. The expected monthly rates were set using the monthly average volume of 15,500 shown in the graph. Also, the graph indicates the actual volume is ahead of plan increasing 11,000 in January to 22,000 in December. After the first quarter, with a perfect forecast equal to the eventual actual results, the team should be pleased with the Q1 results and trend.

Here is where the residual train sometimes goes off the rails. After the first quarter, the cost team analyzed the results. Assuming the costs are highly fixed and have no variance, the chargeback is under-recovered. Why? The average volumes for the first quarter shown in Figure 2.21 are only 12,000 versus an expected average of 15,500. Therefore, on average the chargeback system under-recovered 3,500 units at the expected rate each month. The total Q1 under-recovery is 10,500 units multiplied by the expected rate.

Time to push out a residual and increase the chargeback rate, right? Absolutely not. If anything, the correct response to these actual results and trend is to *decrease* the chargeback rate. However, many inexperienced cost/chargeback teams do just the opposite by pushing out the residual and increasing the chargeback rate.

Let's play out what would happen in the above example if the residual was recovered after Q1 and the chargeback rate was increased by approximately 25% to cover this difference between the expected 15,500 average units and the Q1 12,000 average units. At all subsequent quarterly residual analysis and "correction" opportunities, the chargeback will be over-recovered and the chargeback rate will be decreased because the Q2, Q3 and full-year average volumes will be progressively larger.

To avoid this situation, it is imperative to use the forecasts and, if they are not available or deemed accurate, linear regression to determine the annual volume and chargeback impact. Using the average of the actual results without regard to the forecast will, in many cases, result in multiple residual and chargeback rate adjustments.

To monitor your team's effectiveness at preventing this type of bipolar recovery situation, monitor the number of chargeback rates that have been lowered and later raised, or conversely, raised and later lowered within the same fiscal year. This is can be an indication of not using forecasts, having unexpectedly poor forecasts, or having expectedly poor forecasts without good linear regression to compensate for these known deficiencies.

Cost Plus versus Market Pricing

As a general rule, I do not argue against Nobel prize-winning concepts —whether it is Albert Einstein's $e = mc^2$ or Milton Friedman's "charge what the market will bear" (market pricing). That is why it is so perplexing to see companies employing cost plus pricing models. The battle is over; cost plus lost. Did someone not get the memo? If they did not attend the Nobel Prize ceremony in 1976, did they happen to see the front page *Wall Street Journal* article on March 27, 2007?[1]

Cost plus not only suboptimizes shareholder value by not charging enough for highly-valued products, it encourages the sales force and product managers to manipulate accurate cost assignments to obtain an artificially low cost plus prices. In turn, their revenue numbers look great and they get a tidy compensation while often destroying shareholder value.

As an example of how much value can be generated using market pricing, let's examine cell phone ringtones. The common price point for a ringtone is 99 cents. If the actual cost of the ringtone, including delivery, is five cents, the profit margin per ringtone is 1,880%! Not bad for a multi-billion dollar worldwide industry that did not even exist twenty years ago. The cost has nothing to do with the price. If cost plus mentality had been used to set the price with a "hefty" 60% margin, resulting in a price of eight cents, billions of dollars of shareholder profits would be left on the table.

In my experience, weak product managers and pricing groups use costs as an excuse for a high price. Do not tolerate this behavior. Price and cost are independent. At best, cost plus can help identify a minimum acceptable price. If a company uses a "minimum acceptable price" approach to the market the shareholders will receive minimal return. Personally, I do not look to invest in minimally profitable companies.

NOTE

1. "Seeking Perfect Prices, CEO Tears Up the Rules," *Wall Street Journal*, March 27, 2007.

CHAPTER 3

Implementing ABC

I hear and I forget. I see and I remember. I do and I understand.
—Confucius

ABC IMPLEMENTATION GUIDING PRINCIPLES

A best practice in project management for any formal project is a kick-off session. A kick-off session brings the stakeholders together to understand the high-level project objectives, the ground rules for the project team and, in many cases, meet each other for the first time. The following guiding principles, shown in Figure 3.1 are sample ground rules of an ABC/M implementations.

In case you choose to use the guiding principles in Figure 3.1, here is a little "color" behind each of the principles.

- **Start with the Customers.** This point is driven home several times throughout this book for good reason. ABM in financial services is most effective if the ABC design and implementation is understood, supported, championed, and used by product and customer segment managers. Secondarily, the Finance team needs to understand and use the model to drive change. What information and reports do they need to improve the product and customer profitability?

- **Never choose the tool first. Future state requirements should not be limited by current state tools, processes, or**

ABC/M Project Guiding Principles

- **Start with the Customers.**

  Customers → Output → Process → Input → Source

- **Never choose the tool first. Future state requirements should not be limited by current state tools, processes, or structures.**
- **Use outside comparisons for guidance, but not to limit creativity.**
- **Start with the assumption that everyone made the best decisions in the past with the best available information at that time. There is no "blame" for any past decisions.**
- **Do not let "best" get in the way of "better." Getting to the future state is often an iterative process.**
- **Remember, ABC/M is primarily about business insight and improvements, not accounting. Cost accounting is the means to the ends.**
- **Always make sure the proposed approach will produce the desired result for ABC/M's three primary stakeholders:**
  1. **Line of Business Consumers**
     - ✓ **Product Managers**
     - ✓ **Finance Managers**
  2. **Support Area Providers**
  3. **Cost Accounting Advisors, Implementers, Caretakers, Analysts**

FIGURE 3.1 ABC/M Guiding Principles

structures. Don't become a "fool with a tool." Determine your requirements prior to tool selection. The requirements will drive the tool selection, not the other way around. Just as architectural genius Frank Lloyd Wright stated, "Form follows function." Similarly, tool selection should follow the function definition (requirements).

- **Use outside comparisons for guidance, but not to limit creativity.** Many times during the early phases of an ABC implementation, you will hear, "Well, that is not the way financial services company XYZ implemented ABC." While it is great to have that competitive insight, the team should be encouraged to be even better than XYZ. Data sources, organizational structure, strategy, or available tools impacted XYZ's activity-based costing implementation. Strive to implement the best solution for your company—hopefully, the best solution in the industry (or even the best solution across industries!).

- **Start with the assumption that everyone made the best decisions in the past with the best available information at that time. There is no "blame" for any past decisions.** The blame game is pointless and counterproductive. It only serves to divide your team over rehashed issues. Situations change over time. People become more experienced and knowledgeable. Just move on without the blame.

    It is important, however, to discuss and understand the reasons behind any past failures of any costing, activity-based costing, and performance improvement initiatives to determine mitigating actions for your current implementation. It is best to have these discussions on a one-on-one basis to avoid any unnecessary conflicts. At the kick-off, let your team know that you will be soliciting their feedback and advice in the near future.

- **Do not let "best" get in the way of "better." Getting to the future state is often an iterative process.** Your team will need to work in three different states: the current state, the near state, and the future state. The current state is today's reality. The future state is the ABC/M vision which may take years to accomplish. The near state is the next iteration of improvement. For example, while the ABC team's future-state vision may be a heavy graph-based online analytical drill-down for all product income statements, the near state may need to be a spreadsheet drill-down of the same information. Or while 90% automated driver collection will be part of the future state vision, the near state may need 50% automated driver collection—which is quite an improvement over the current state of 0% automated driver collection.

- **Remember, ABC/M is primarily about business insight and improvements, not accounting. Cost accounting is the means to the ends.** ABC practitioners consistently agree with this advice, yet companies continue to try to push ABC through the Finance and Accounting groups—primarily through the CFO or Controller.

Since lines of business (LOBs) are often given a high degree of autonomy regarding products and customer service, there is not an initial corporate-wide push for ABC outside of the finance community. The CEO and heads of the business lines need to recognize the potential of ABC/M and own the outcomes of the project. ABC/M should be in the annual goals for the business line leaders.

■ **Always make sure the proposed approach will produce the desired result for ABC/M's three primary stakeholders: LOB Consumers, Support Area Providers, and Cost Accounting.** In the quest to provide the product managers with the ultimate ABC/M solution, remember to include other key stakeholders such as:

■ **Pricing managers** help price for the unique customer behaviors and understand how to influence customer behavior through pricing. Product managers need to have full accountability for product income statements.

■ **Customer segment managers** understand the customer base and could use insights from ABC/M to grow (or intentionally shrink) subsegments. Similar to product managers, the customer segment managers need to have full accountability for customer segment income statements.

■ **Incentive plan managers** drive sales personnel behavior through the incentive plans. This group of individuals can use ABC/M to help identify and correct misalignments between incentive plans and actual results. In a bank, for example, if the incentive plan strongly pushes sales personnel to open new checking accounts regardless of size, it is amazing how many $1 checking accounts are opened each month.

■ **Finance managers** are responsible for the overall financial well-being of the corporation and can be extremely valuable for initiatives across lines of business (LOBs).

■ **Support areas** provide dual roles through ABC/M implementation. First, they are responsible for identifying and improving the profitability of products and customers through the identification and implementation of process improvements. Second, they are jointly responsible for working with the LOB managers to implement improvements identified solely by the LOBs.

- **Cost accounting** is responsible for the brass-tacks implementation of ABC and generally the ongoing maintenance. Constructing an unsustainable ABC/M solution will not only damage ABC/M in the eyes of the users, but in the eyes of the cost accounting group, too.

MODEL RULES, ASSUMPTIONS, AND DESIGN DOCUMENTS

In many cases, the implementation of any new process, including ABC/M, starts as a nebulous gray cloud. As the change champion and implementer, you will focus a large part of your energy on turning the gray cloud into black and white concrete concepts, plans, and benefits. Two documents assist this effort. The first document is created early in the implementation and contains the high-level ABC model rules and assumptions. The document is generally not lengthy (2 to 10 pages, depending on the size and complexity of the implementation), but addresses the larger directional options of the implementation. The Appendix at the end of this book contains a small sample document from an ABC implementation at an Information Technology (IT) shared services organization.

The second important document is the ABC design document. This is a reflection of all of the design decisions incorporated into the ABC implementation. This document examines the design of each of the ABC levels—resources, resource drivers, activities, activity drivers, and cost objects. Like all documentation, it is tempting to build the ABC/M system without the ABC design document. Don't. While you and your team are intimately familiar with the inner workings of the design, the purpose of the ABC design document is to inform future ABC maintenance team members how and why the team designed the model the way it did. The ABC design document also speeds up the on-boarding process for new team members added during the ABC implementation.

The rest of this chapter focuses on topics that are generally addressed in either or both of these documents.

DRIVER DECISIONS

The accuracy and applicability of the resource and activity drivers are the largest determinants of the accuracy of the ABC system. If you have accurate counts of drivers that truly represent the work, you will create an accurate ABC model.

Full-Time Equivalents versus Percent of Time

Commonly, some portion of the resource costs are driven by how personnel spend their time. Time studies and surveys of the employees performing the activities are the most effective ways of determining the base personnel resource drivers. Resource idle time can be incorporated into both time studies and surveys. For example, a time and motion study at bank branches revealed that approximately 30% of the teller time was spent waiting for a customer to come in the door (idle capacity). This activity was placed in the ABC model as "Wait for Customer" and was subsequently targeted for improvement. Similarly staffed branches were ranked based on their idle capacity. In general, branches with higher staffing levels were more efficient than lower staffing levels since there is a minimum number of people required to keep a branch open at all times. Outliers to this correlation were targeted for improvement.

Time studies involving wands and barcodes can be a very accurate method of driving costs to activities and subsequently cost objects. They are most appropriately used in areas without a great degree of activity time variance. Areas ideal for time studies include servicing areas (including branches) and operations. Time studies are not appropriate in areas with a high degree of customization and, therefore, variability in activity times. Areas not ideal for time studies include corporate sales due to the complexity and variability of deals and IT development due to the uniqueness of each project.

Another good source of personnel resource hours is a company's labor tracking system. This type of system is more common in IT units within the organization. Usually, these systems track the hours worked by task/activity for each employee by project or application.

Regardless of the method used to capture resource drivers, the final personnel resource drivers should be shown in terms of full-time equivalents (FTEs). While capturing the data in hours or percent of time is perfectly acceptable from a mathematics standpoint, executive audiences prefer to see the data in terms of FTEs. It provides a common basis for effort-based comparisons throughout the corporation.

Best Drivers

Best (or ideal) drivers are those drivers that most accurately reflect the work request/cost relationship in Figure 2.17. Additionally, the best drivers are automated and are updated on a monthly basis. As you build the activity dictionary and driver dictionary, clearly identify the best drivers, sources, and frequency. Activity and driver dictionaries are described later in this chapter.

Proxy Drivers

Sometimes the best drivers do not exist or are not automated. In these cases, "Don't let best get in the way of better." As the name implies, proxy (or surrogate) drivers can be used to represent the best drivers. The key to proxy drivers is that they behave directionally the same as the best drivers: The more closely correlated the proxy drivers are to the best drivers, the more accurate the ABC model. For example, if the best activity driver for Clear Checks is the number of checks processed for each product, the proxy driver may be the number of transaction accounts for each product. As the number of transaction accounts increases or decreases, the number of checks processed should increase or decrease, too.

Often, the ABC implementation team will use proxy drivers in the initial implementation of ABC and then migrate to best drivers in subsequent iterations. This approach improves the "speed to value" of ABC implementations by generating initial directionally-accurate results, while improving future accuracy and automation.

Weighted Drivers

When the amount of resources required to complete a particular activity varies materially by product or other cost object, you have two choices. As one alternative, you can break the activity down into more discrete activities. For example, Setup Loan could be broken into Setup Unsecured Loan and Setup Secured Loan if the differentiating resource use is based on whether or not the loan is secured.

A second alternative is creating driver weights by cost object. In the above example, if secured loans take twice as much effort to set up, each of the activity drivers for secured loans would have a weight of 2. So, if I set up ten unsecured loans (weighted volume: $10 \times 1 = 10$) and five secured loans (weighted volume: $5 \times 2 = 10$), my activity costs would be assigned equally between these to products from a single Setup Loan activity.

A word of caution: While weights are useful for minimizing the overall number of activities, do not go overboard. If the "exception" weights are not at least 50% (1.5 ×) larger or 50% (0.5 ×) smaller than the default, do not waste your energy. Use a standard weight of 1 for minor differences.

ATTRIBUTE DECISIONS

"Attributes" in ABC parlance refer to the characteristics of resources and activities. Good ABC systems use attributes to establish different reporting dimensions to facilitate cost analysis and insight. Some of the most common dimensions are discussed in this section—time attributes of the cost (fixed/variable), quality attributes of the activities, value attributes of the activities, channel attributes of the activities, and capacity attributes. The power of thoughtfully-defined attributes cannot be overstated. Attributes are tremendously valuable for providing insight into the ABC model results and enabling ABM. They add color to the black-and-white picture of raw ABC results.

Fixed and Variable Attributes

All costs are variable in the long term. Buildings and equipment can be sold and long-term contracts can be renegotiated. The notion of fixed and variable costs is directional, not absolute. As a rule of thumb, consider fixed costs those costs which are unlikely to be changed in less than one year as a result of ABM improvements or moderate changes in volume—property, plant, and equipment, for example. With moderate changes in volume, these costs generally do not change. Conversely, variable costs are likely to be changed in less than one year as a result of ABM improvements or moderate changes in volume.

In the ABC model, each of the resource cost pools can have an associated Fixed or Variable attribute. With the traceback capability available in ABC modeling tools, both activities and cost objects can be viewed in terms of fixed and variable cost components just by tagging the resource cost pools. Figure 3.2 shows an example of assigning fixed/variable attributes to resource cost pools.

During one implementation of ABC, we created another attribute label within fixed/variable called Immediate. Immediate was used to represent costs that had a one-for-one relationship with the activity drivers. For example, in Figure 3.2, Postage and Supplies was considered an immediate expense in the Statements department. For every incremental increase or decrease in printed statements, there was an immediate increase or decrease to the required postage and supplies. The Immediate label helped the team identify "quick hit" ABM ideas.[1]

Direct Expense	Attributes
Personnel Expenses	Variable
Occupancy	Fixed
Furniture, Equipment, and Software	Fixed
Marketing and Public Relations	Variable
Postage and Supplies	Variable
Telephone	Variable
Travel and Entertainment	Variable
Other Third Party Service Fees	Variable
Losses/(Recoveries)	Variable
Other	Fixed
IS Projects	Variable
Intangible Asset Amortization	Fixed

FIGURE 3.2   Assignment of Fixed/Variable Attributes

Cost of Quality and Cost of Poor Quality Attributes

The quality movement in the United States, driven by Deming, Juran, and Crosby, began in earnest in the early 1980s. It was not uncommon for companies to improve their bottom lines 15–20% by "doing it right the first time" or DIRTFT (pronounced "dirt foot"). The quality movement has taken on a couple of different forms since the 1980s including Total Quality Management (TQM), Six Sigma, and Lean Manufacturing (or even Lean Six Sigma).

Common steps when implementing a corporate-wide quality program include identifying and prioritizing improvements. ABC attributes can assist in this effort. Figure 3.3, adapted from *Activity-Based Cost Management: An Executive's Guide* by Gary Cokins, shows a recommended structure for tagging activities with Cost of Quality (COQ) attributes. Every activity should be tagged with one of five COQ attributes: Error-free, Prevention, Assurance, Reactive-Internal, or Reactive-External. A Six Sigma program office can utilize these attributes to identify and prioritize improvement projects.

In Figure 3.3, notice how the Six Sigma concept of Cost of Poor Quality (COPQ) with the focus on Prevention, Assurance, and Reactive

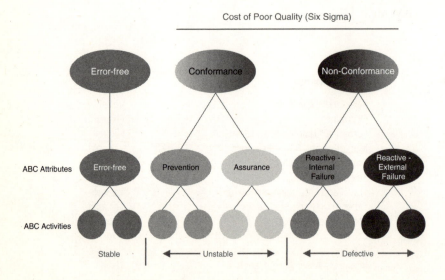

FIGURE 3.3 Integrating Cost of Quality into Six Sigma

is a subset of the whole COQ attributes. Also, notice how the COQ attributes are sorted left to right from the highest quality attributes (error-free) attributes to the lowest quality attributes (activities performed to respond to errors found by your customers).

The combination of COQ activity attributes and Fixed/Variable resource attributes is very powerful. If you want relatively quick payback by improving low-quality activities, sort your activity model information by the largest variable costs for reactive external failure activities.

As with any of the attributes, before you use them, develop a solid definition for each attribute. Gary Cokins' book[2] is an excellent resource for developing attribute definitions and there is no need to reinvent his efforts in this book.

Value-Added and Non-Value-Added Attributes

Value-Added (VA) and Non-Value-Added (NVA) attributes are frequently used in ABC to link activities to process reengineering analysis. If you choose to use VA/NVA attributes, remember to develop solid definitions first. Once again, Gary Cokins' book is an excellent resource for developing these definitions.

In my experience, the COQ attributes are more powerful and less contentious than the VA/NVA attributes. Given the choice, use COQ attributes instead of VA/NVA attributes. Once, as part of an ABC implementation, I simplified the VA/NVA concept by assigning VA attributes to all Error-free activities and NVA to all other activities. While this method is certainly not perfect, it is directionally correct and very straightforward.

Channel Attributes

Depending on the complexity of the industry and the ABC model, it may be necessary to use a channel attribute. For example, in banking, are the activities exclusively associated with branch, call center, ATM, or online? If revenue is associated with each of these channels, the profitability of each channel can be quantified and compared. Is the ATM channel more profitable for your client base? This type of information is useful for determining channel investment levels and investments/divestitures within channels. Should we invest in more ATMs or branches? More specifically, which types of ATMs or branches require investment?

Unused Capacity Modeling Attributes

In the Standard Rates section of Chapter 2, we reviewed the concept of standard rates and unused (excess) capacity. Theoretically, you can tag all of the activities with a Used or Unused capacity attribute. This attribute information can be used to demonstrate the total cost of unused capacity for the organization. Given the real world complexities of standard rates and unused capacity, I never used this attribute throughout an ABC model. Instead, unused capacity activities should be determined using time studies, tracked by the ABC/M team, and reported without the use of attributes.

LEVEL OF DETAIL DECISIONS

Einstein famously stated, "Keep things as simple as possible—but no simpler." This holds true for ABC, as well. The difficulty with ABC is taking something very complex and making it appear simple and intuitive to the users. You have three important weapons in the battle for simplicity: hierarchies, costing policies, and technology tools (for faster driver extraction and multidimensional reporting).

Hierarchies of Resources, Activities, and Cost Objects

Hierarchies allow your ABC information to be organized for easier analysis. The ABC model may contain thousands of cost center feeds (by general ledger account) into various resource pools. The activity module may contain hundreds of activities, organized by subprocesses and processes. The cost object module may contain hundreds of products, organized by product lines.

Figure 3.4 shows the various hierarchies of each ABC model module.

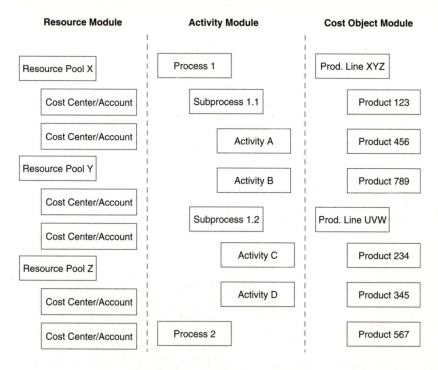

FIGURE 3.4 ABC Module Hierarchies

In the resource model, it is common to roll up the cost center/ account combinations into resource pools unique and meaningful to ABC/M: Personnel, Personnel-Related, and Equipment, for example. This method results in roughly 6 to 10 standard resource pools for each area modeled. However, if the company has done a good job controlling the general ledger hierarchy, you may utilize existing general ledger roll-ups for the resource pools. During one implementation, my team used the existing 18 general ledger roll-ups and a metadata tool to minimize the maintenance of the ABC model. The maintenance effort saved was well worth the additional setup in the ABC model to utilize eighteen resource pools, many of which had duplicative drivers and would have been combined by ABC purists.

For some models, there may be more than two levels in the hierarchy. I recommend three levels in the activity hierarchy: processes, subprocesses, and activities. For example, in banking, the process level could simply be Sell, Maintain, and Transact. All activities for a commercial bank fall into one of these three processes. Subprocesses that roll up to Transact may include: Add Funds (Credit), Subtract Funds (Debit), and Inquire. Within the Add Funds subprocess are all of the necessary activities required to add funds into the account. In most cases, there is not an existing standard activity hierarchy that can be used for the ABC implementation. In contrast to the resource and product hierarchies, the activity hierarchy is, in all likelihood, owned and maintained by the ABC/M team.

Finally, for product hierarchies, leverage the existing product hierarchies at the company. Individual products probably roll up to product lines. In some cases, these product lines may roll up to product groups or families. Do not re-invent the wheel here. Once again, this type of metadata (hierarchies) can be maintained outside the ABC model and fed to the reporting tool.

Technically, it is not necessary to keep the activity or product hierarchy information within the ABC model. It is only necessary to keep this hierarchical information within the ABC/M reporting tool. This may or may not be the same tool as the ABC modeling tool.

One useful technique to consider is "intelligent" number of activities and drivers. For example, make the activity numbers nine digits and the driver numbers eight digits. Use the first digit to differentiate between shared services activities (1–4) and front office activities (5–9). This intelligent numbering will help your team interpret raw ABC data quicker.

Costing Policies: The $500,000 or 5 FTE Rule

Inevitably, during your activity interviews, you will find people that believe the ABC/M interviews are a justification of their jobs. These people typically list everything they do as an "activity," regardless of size. They seem to say, "Look! I do fifteen different things. See how valuable I am?" One way I have found to avoid confusing tasks with activities is to set a floor threshold of relevance for the activities. Typically, I require that all activities cost at least $500,000 annually or require a minimum of five FTEs. The $500,000 or 5 FTE rule is employed company wide.

Even with this rule, most ABC models are overengineered (have too many activities) from the start and require a "clean-up" iteration to reduce the number of activities and drivers. Simple policies like the "$500,000 or 5 FTE" rule will reduce this clean-up effort.

Exceptions

Unfortunately, there are a few exceptions to some policies. Exceptions include activities that are intended to be driven to zero or minimized. These activities are typically rework activities resulting from COPQ activities. Additionally, some activities may be driven down due to technology changes. The owning area may want to monitor the reduction of these activity costs over time.

TOOLS

There are a few tools commonly used in a fully-automated and easily-maintained ABC/M system. Depending on the configuration, you may use several vendors or, as the software industry continues to consolidate, only one. This section provides a brief explanation of tools and general functionality required. The tools and vendors may come and go, but the general functionality required has not changed much over the past ten years.

Modeling Tools

The centerpiece of the ABC system is the modeling tool. Think of it as the calculator for determining the activity and product costs. The ABC model is fed a lot of data and produces information. Several software vendors, including most Enterprise Resource Management (ERP) suites, provide ABC modeling tools. Personally, I have had good experiences with both SAS ABM and BusinessObject's Metify tools.

Extract, Transform, and Load Tools

Extract, Transform, and Load (ETL) tools are lifesavers for moving the data from the multitude of sources into the ABC modeling tool and from the ABC modeling tool to Online Analytical Processing (OLAP) reporting, if necessary. The purpose of the ETL tools is to extract data from a source database, perform transformations (including mathematical and logical transformations) required by the target database, and load the target database. ETL tools replace the manual, monotonous, and error-prone manual efforts historically performed for monthly costing system loads. Common stand-alone tools in this arena are Informatica's Powermart/Powercenter and Ab Initio. Additionally, some ABC tool vendors such as SAS have integrated some ETL functionality to make life easier.

Metadata Tools

To establish and maintain a "single source of the truth" for the hierarchies used in ABC, I recommend a metadata management tool. In layman's terms, metadata is information *about* the information sources including definitions, locations, and hierarchies. For example, metadata is data that indicates that the Number of Withdrawals is a field in the Demand Deposit table represented as a short positive integer and was last changed yesterday. One of the most popular metadata tools, Razza, was purchased by Hyperion in early 2005.

Reporting Tools

The reporting tool is absolutely essential to your roll-out and adoption of ABM. The reporting tool should be an OLAP engine powerful enough to quickly slice and dice the data to provide meaningful, timely analysis. Additionally, the reporting tool needs to be simple and accessible to the masses. With these two requirements in mind, you may not be satisfied with the reporting capabilities directly from the ABC tool. However, there are many solutions offered in this space including those offered by Hyperion (Oracle), Cognos (IBM), and Microsoft. Find the reporting solution that best fits your end-users' needs and your IT architecture.

ACTIVITY AND DRIVER DICTIONARIES

Even though I have yet to meet an ABC practitioner that enjoys documentation, we all realize how essential it is to the long-term success of

ABC/M. Major components of the ABC/M documentation are the activity and driver dictionaries. As the names imply, the activity and driver dictionaries define the activities, activity drivers, and resource drivers.

Each activity in the activity dictionary should contain the following:

- Activity number and name
- Business area and owner
- Activity driver used
- Tasks that define the activity
- ABC modeler/interviewer (ABC Team Contact)
- Last update name and date

The companion website (see page xix) contains an example of a report from an activity dictionary database. Note that all of the data fields are not shown in this particular report, but all of the fields are contained in the activity dictionary.

Each driver in the driver dictionary should contain the following:

- Driver number and name
- Source type: system-generated or manual
- Source system
- Data source owner
- Description of the data source including any data transformation
- ABC modeler/interviewer
- Last update name and date

The activity and driver dictionaries are highly functional and should be refreshed at least annually. The dictionaries are usually developed in spreadsheets and then imported into a small database repository for ease of maintenance.

As mentioned earlier in the chapter, "intelligent" numbering of activities and drivers is a useful technique to employ to make the raw data more intuitive. Use different alphanumeric lengths and ranges to differentiate resources, activities, cost objects, resource drivers, and activity drivers.

PUTTING IT ALL TOGETHER: AN ABC EXAMPLE

Now that we have finally gotten all of the basics out of the way, what does it look like? Hopefully, if a picture is truly worth a thousand words, this section will be better understood with fewer words and a simplified example.

Step 1: The Set-Up

Figure 3.5 shows the focus of the example on two activities, Process Documents and Open Accounts within the Sales process. These two activities support four products, Trade, Hybrid, Traditional IRA, and Roth IRA, within two LOBs, Retail and Wealth Management. The two activities are assigned to the products and LOBs based on the number of new accounts.

Step 2: Driving Equally Weighted Costs

Figure 3.6 shows that 200 new accounts drive the Process Document costs to the four products within the two LOBs. Like most activities, all weights are equal, indicating that there is no material difference in the effort required to process the documents for any of the product/LOB combinations. The expected unit cost ($5.00 per new account) is simply the activity cost divided by the number of new accounts.

Step 3: Equally Weighted Results

Figure 3.7 shows product/LOB results of the new account assignments from Process Documents. The entire $1,000 is driven to the product/LOB combinations.

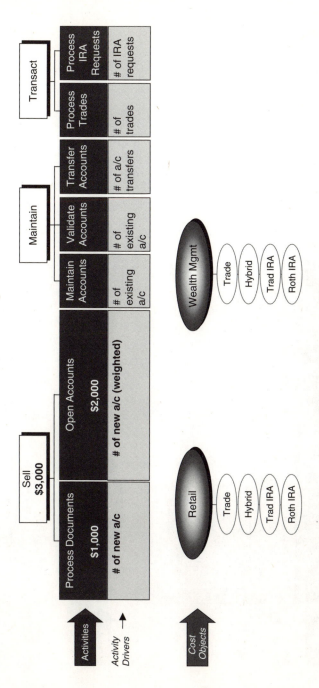

FIGURE 3.5 ABC Example—Set-up

73

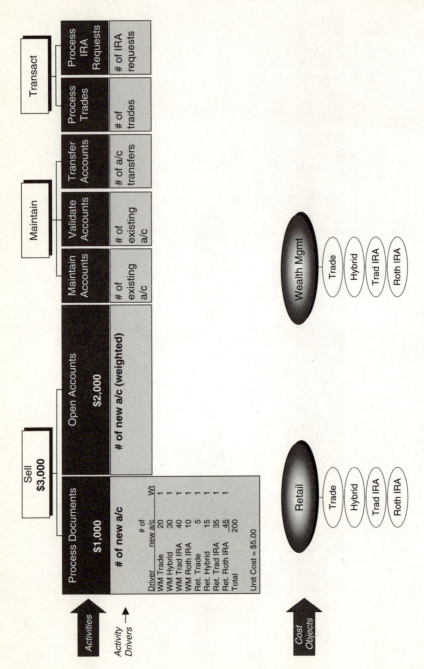

FIGURE 3.6 ABC Example—Driving Equally Weighted Costs

74

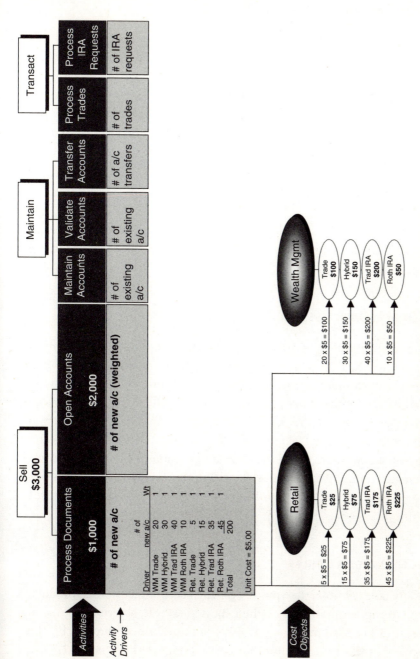

FIGURE 3.7 ABC Example—Process Documents Results

Step 4: Driving Differently Weighted Costs

Now it gets a bit trickier. Figure 3.8 shows the same 200 new accounts driving Open Account costs differently to the four products within the two LOBs. In this case, the weights are not equal, indicating that there is a material difference in the effort required to open the Trade and Traditional IRA accounts. The weighted expected unit cost ($7.62 per weighted new account) is equal to the activity cost divided by the total weighted number of new accounts.

Step 5: Final Results

Finally, Figure 3.9 shows product/LOB total results of the new account assignments from the Sales process. The entire $3,000 is driven to the product/LOB combinations.

A Chargeback Rate Table

Once all expected rates are calculated in the ABC model, the rate information can be exported to create a chargeback rate table. Rather than moving rates significantly from month-to-month, the rate table with quarterly true-ups forces an emphasis on ABC/M explanations of driver variances. Figure 3.10 demonstrates a simplified version of an expected rate table. While not all product/LOB/activity rates are shown in this figure, all of them would be contained in the actual implementation. Also, technically, the product and LOB dimensions would be separate, although they are combined for simplicity in this figure.

A Customer's Costs

At any point in time, the volumes for each account, customer, product, or LOB can be multiplied by the expected rates to determine costs. In Figure 3.11, customer Jane Smith's volumes are multiplied by the expected rates to determine her costs. Jane Smith costs $132.39 to serve.

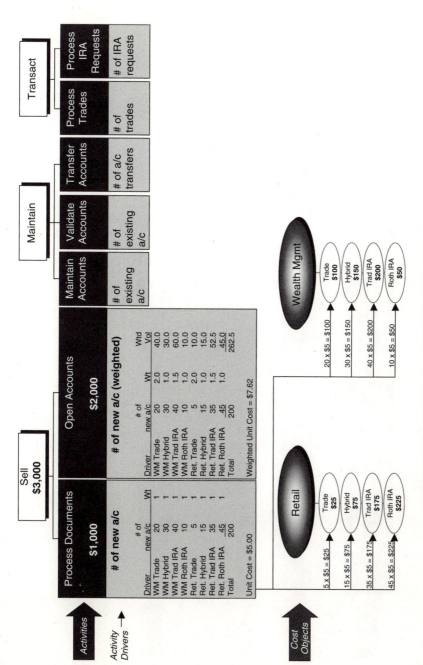

FIGURE 3.8 ABC Example—Driving Differently Weighted Costs

77

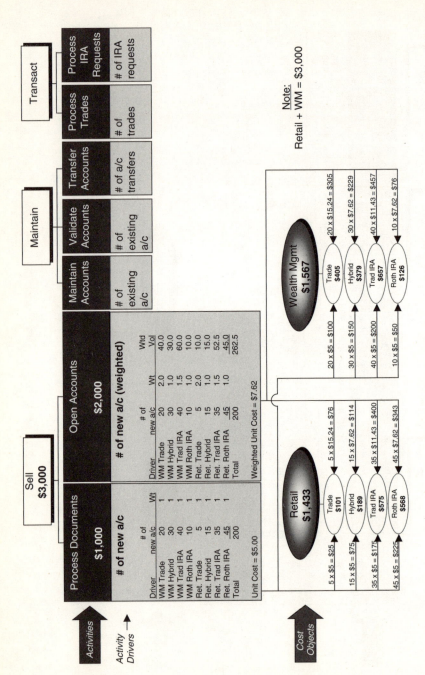

FIGURE 3.9 ABC Example—Final Results

78

Expected Rate Table

Activities	WM Trade	WM Hybrid	WM Trad IRA	WM Roth IRA	Ret. Trade
Process Documents	$5.00	$5.00	$5.00	$5.00	$5.00
Open Accounts	$15.24	$7.62	$11.43	$7.62	$15.24
Maintain Accounts	$x	$x	$x	$x	$x
Validate Accounts	$y	$y	$y	$y	$y
Process IRA Requests	-	-	$z	$z	-

Products

FIGURE 3.10   Chargeback Rate Table

The Costing Cube

As discussed in the section on Reporting, most sophisticated ABC/M implementations use an OLAP reporting tool as the engine. Figure 3.12 depicts this type of multidimensional reporting in a cube structure. The dimensions are activities, customers, and products. Once again, in an actual ABC implementation, the product dimension shown would be a pure dimension and, therefore, would not contain any LOB information.

Expected Rate Table

Activities \ Products	WM Trade	WM Hybrid	WM Trad IRA	WM Roth IRA	Ret. Trade
Process Documents	$5.00	$5.00	$5.00	$5.00	$5.00
Open Accounts	$15.24	$7.62	$11.43	$7.62	$15.24
Maintain Accounts	$x	$x	$x	$x	$x
Validate Accounts	$y	$y	$y	$y	$y
Process IRA Requests	-	-	$z	$z	-

$\times$

Jane Smith Activities (Volume)

Activities \ Products	WM Trade	WM Hybrid	WM Trad IRA	WM Roth IRA	Ret. Trade
Process Documents	3	0	1	2	0
Open Accounts	3	0	1	2	0
Maintain Accounts	0	0	0	0	0
Validate Accounts	0	0	0	0	0
Process IRA Requests	0	0	0	0	0

=

Jane Smith Rate x Volume

Activities \ Products	WM Trade	WM Hybrid	WM Trad IRA	WM Roth IRA	Ret. Trade
Process Documents	$15.00	0	$5.00	$10.00	0
Open Accounts	$45.72	0	$11.43	$15.24	0
Maintain Accounts	0	0	0	0	0
Validate Accounts	0	0	0	0	0
Process IRA Requests	0	0	0	0	0

Jane Smith's Total Cost:

$132.39

FIGURE 3.11 A Customer's Costs

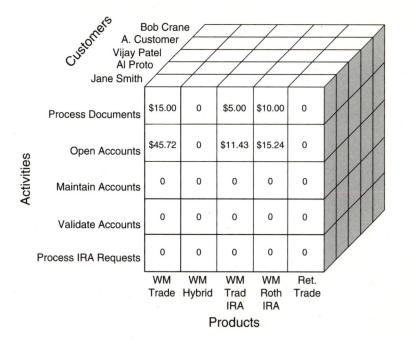

FIGURE 3.12 The Costing Cube

NOTES

1. In order to be consistent with the Association for Financial Professionals, you may choose to use the terms Fixed, Variable, and Semi-variable instead of Fixed, Immediate, and Variable, respectively.
2. Gary Cokins. *Activity-Based Cost Management: An Executive's Guide* (Hoboken, NJ: John Wiley & Sons, 2001).

CHAPTER **4**

Implementing ABM

Plan your work. Work your plan. Your plan will work.

—Anonymous

STRUCTURING THE ORGANIZATION AND PROCESS FOR SUCCESS

As stated earlier in the book, the goal of an ABC/M implementation is to drive ABM value to the bottom line. Strong project management is required for ABC and ABM implementations. Depending on the scope and complexity of the efforts, strong program management is required, too. Clearly, an enterprise-wide implementation of ABM at a multibillion dollar corporation requires both program and project management.

Where do you find strong program and project managers? Look for them in areas that frequently deliver programs and projects: Information Technology (IT), Operations, Product Management, and Six Sigma groups. For the program manager, look for someone that manages project managers, understands the project life cycle, understands how to align the organization, implements change management, and communicates well. If your organization keeps a record of Project Management Professional (PMP) certifications, seek these people. While the

PMP is not a guarantee of wisdom, execution, and success, it certainly improves your odds. Personally, many of the tools and techniques I use during an ABC/M implementation come from years of experience and reinforcement from employers, clients, peers, and courses taken to earn and maintain PMP certification.

The remainder of this section describes eight proven steps to implement ABM within your organization.

Create the Charter with Scope, Goals, Milestones, and Timelines

In any program or project, you need to define the objectives, scope, resources, and timing to demonstrate that you understand where you're going and how you plan to get there. These pieces of information are contained in the ABM charter.

The ABM charter is especially useful for getting people on the "same page." The sponsor of the ABC/M initiative should be identified in the charter and must agree to all aspects of the charter. The ABM charter forces some potentially difficult conversations regarding the objectives, scope, resources, and timing. A standard project management theory called the "triple constraint" theory states that three major constraints define a project's potential: scope, resources, and timing. Two of the constraints must be defined to determine the third variable. For example, if you are constrained by having ten people (resources) and three months (timing), there is a limited amount of work (scope) that can be undertaken. Similarly, if you have been given defined scope and timing, you'll be able to determine the resources required for successful execution.

When should the ABM charter be created? Ideally, the initial ABM charter is created as part of the ABC/M kick-off. The ABM charter is refined periodically throughout the ABC implementation as better information becomes available. Once ABM projects are set up and value is being driven to the bottom line, it is no longer necessary to update the ABM charter. It is not a "living document" for the entire ABM implementation. The ABM charter is best used as a pre-execution guide and for post-execution analysis.

Establish a Core ABM Organization

The core ABM organization is focused on driving bottom line results using the ABC data. Keep the organization small and talented. As with any improvement organization, the core ABM team will need to demonstrate their value quarterly and annually. Any improvement group should return five to ten times their salaries to the bottom line annually. Beware of employees that believe PowerPoint preparations and presentations are "execution." This is not a statement against PowerPoint, but an acknowledgement of the fact that after a decade of fancy presentations, some employees believe that making a business case is the equivalent of implementing the business case. This is simply not true. Business cases, grand visions, and strategies are worthless without execution. Find talented executors with a variety of backgrounds. The core group should be capable of augmenting individual ABM projects with standard project management skills to drive execution.

Baseline the Current State of In-Scope ABM

In order to demonstrate the value of the ABM initiatives, current state (or As Is) baselines must be created. This is a standard step in improvement projects. For example, the Measure phase in Six Sigma's DMAIC (Define, Measure, Analyze, Improve, Control) process establishes a baseline for future improvement validation.

There are fundamental differences between baselines, benchmarks, and best practices.

- **Baselines** are the measured "current state" of processes or process outputs. Clearly, ABC/M enables baselines through the creation of time-based resource drivers, activity costs, activity drivers, product costs, and customer costs. Baseline ABC/M to demonstrate future success.
- **Benchmarks** can be either internal or external comparisons of processes or process outputs usually within the same industry. Internal benchmarks are particularly useful for ABC/M implementations when the same process is performed in several geographies. When we implemented ABC/M at a large insurance

company, we discovered one region was much more efficient re-solving PC problems. The reason, we quickly realized, was that only this region used a standard checklist for problem debugging and resolution. The other regions used a more "shoot from the hip" approach which was generally not as successful. External benchmarks can be problematic. At some level, every company believes they are unique and external comparisons are invalid. Over the years, I have basically thrown in the towel for most external benchmarks because people spend more time arguing about the accuracy and comparability of the data than improving the business.

■ **Best Practices (or Leading Practices)** are generally a cross-industry external comparison of processes or process outputs. In my experience, best practices are less contentious than benchmarks. Due to popular business literature, most people associate best practices behavior with Wal-Mart, Southwest Airlines, Nordstrom's, and McDonald's without a lot of arguing about the data. In most cases, though, the best practices are more of an aspiration, not a hard and fast measurement of success.

Prioritize Projects and Deliver Quick Wins

In the beginning, the ABM team will have more opportunities than it can undertake. Prioritize the ABM projects based on value and ease of implementation (which is highly correlated with speed to value). Use a standard consulting two-by-two matrix like the one shown in Figure 4.1 to prioritize the ABM projects.

At this point, the fully quantified value and project plan (ease) are not known. This is a qualitative assessment of the relative value and implementation effort relative to the other projects in your ABM portfolio. Working with this type of matrix for more than ten years, I recommend focusing on one project at a time and one dimension at a time. Is Project XYZ a large benefit or small benefit? After that question is answered, determine if Project XYZ is easy or difficult to implement. Now move on to the next project.

Once all of the ABM projects are neatly classified on the two-by-two matrix, where do you spend your time and effort? Clearly the

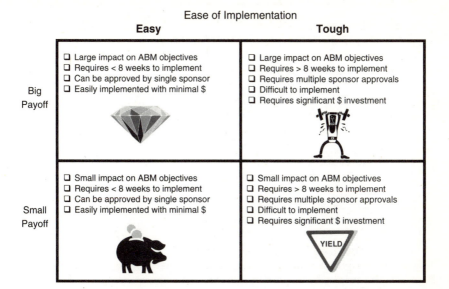

Ease of Implementation

	Easy	Tough
Big Payoff	❑ Large impact on ABM objectives ❑ Requires < 8 weeks to implement ❑ Can be approved by single sponsor ❑ Easily implemented with minimal $	❑ Large impact on ABM objectives ❑ Requires > 8 weeks to implement ❑ Requires multiple sponsor approvals ❑ Difficult to implement ❑ Requires significant $ investment
Small Payoff	❑ Small impact on ABM objectives ❑ Requires < 8 weeks to implement ❑ Can be approved by single sponsor ❑ Easily implemented with minimal $	❑ Small impact on ABM objectives ❑ Requires > 8 weeks to implement ❑ Requires multiple sponsor approvals ❑ Difficult to implement ❑ Requires significant $ investment YIELD

FIGURE 4.1 Two-by-Two ABM Prioritization

small payoff, tough implementation quadrant should be avoided, but the large payoff, tough implementation sure looks tempting. In the beginning, 90% of your effort should be focused on generating easy wins. If the ABM team is fortunate enough to have a large payoff/easy implementation combinations, make these projects your top priority. Next, implement the small payoff/easy implementation combinations. A few hundred thousand dollars here and there . . . and soon you're delivering meaningful improvements to the bottom line!

As the ABM portfolio grows and matures, it may be useful to migrate to more sophisticated project portfolio tools. Some of these tools are discussed later in this chapter.

Why is delivering these quick wins so important? Remember, you're not just implementing improvement in a "frictionless" environment. You are leading change in the organization—the people, the process and, possibly, the technology—and organizations resist change. See Figure 4.2, for a summary of the required steps for leading organizational change identified in John Kotter's book, *Leading Change*. In my experience, Kotter's emphasis on delivering quick wins is right on the money. Public acknowledgement of quick wins inspires the

1. **Establish a sense of urgency**
   - Examine market and competitive realities
   - Identify and discuss crises, potential crises, or major opportunities
2. **Form a powerful guiding coalition**
   - Assemble a group with enough power to lead the change effort
   - Encourage the group to work together as a team
3. **Create a vision**
   - Create a vision to help direct the change effort
   - Develop strategies for achieving that vision
4. **Communicate vision**
   - Use every vehicle possible to communicate the new vision and strategies
   - Teach new behaviors by the example of the guiding coalition
5. **Empower others to act on the vision**
   - Get rid of obstacles to change
   - Change systems or structures that seriously undermine the vision
   - Encourage risk taking and nontraditional ideas, activities, and actions
6. **Plan for and creating short-term wins**
   - Plan for visible performance improvements
   - Create those improvements
   - Recognize and reward employees involved in the improvements
7. **Consolidate improvements and produce still more change**
   - Use increased credibility to change systems, structures, and policies that don't fit the vision
   - Hire, promote, and develop employees who can implement the vision
   - Reinvigorate the process with new projects, themes, and change agents
8. **Institutionalize new approaches**
   - Articulate the connections between the new behaviors and corporate success
   - Develop the means to ensure leadership development and succession

FIGURE 4.2   Eight Steps for Leading Change

Adapted from *Leading Change* by John Kotter (Cambridge, MA: Harvard Business Press, 1996)

ABM team and silences critics. Just remember, make sure the quick win is legitimate: a sustainable, direct outcome of the ABC/M analysis. Otherwise, you may inadvertently cause damage to the long-term reputation of the ABM team.

Design an ABM Project Delivery Process

While the ABM team is delivering quick wins, you need to design the ABM project delivery process. The ABM project delivery process addresses the following:

- **How are projects identified?** Use the ABC findings. Are the projects determined by the project team, the entire organization, a consultant, or all of these? Ideas surfaced through talks with the organization and vetted with an experienced project team or an outside consultant have the greatest chance of success. Public acknowledgement of the idea generators keeps this flow coming to the team.

- **How are projects prioritized?** Senior management will be interested in the ABM team's current and future method for project prioritization. As long as the ABM team delivers results, the prioritization method can be as simple as the two-by-two matrix in shown Figure 4.1.

- **How are project benefits (business cases) created?** The business cases should be created by a combination of the process owners, financial owners (expense and revenue), financial personnel and the ABM team. In the end, the process and financial owners are accountable for the outcome and must be part of the business case development. Beware of the sneaky change champion that commits to implement the project in his area, but commits to benefits on behalf of another area ("If I implement this project in Operations, HR will save millions!" Only HR can sign up for these savings). No one should be allowed to commit another area's savings.

- **Who can approve or reject projects?** How much influence and power does the ABM team have? Since ABM improvements require change, ABM management needs to be entrusted with sufficient influence and power to enable buy-in and overcome undue resistance. In my experience, the most effective method is the creation and use of an ABM Board (discussed in the next step) for approval decisions. As change champions commit to

deliver ABM improvements, they submit implementation notices to the ABM Board, which documents the schedule and
benefits expected.

- ▪ **What individual project delivery methodologies are
  used?** Are all projects treated as Six Sigma projects or is the
  delivery methodology project-dependent? I recommend a
  project-dependent approach to methodology selection. Never
  choose the tool (methodology, in this case) first. A carpenter
  with a single saw in his toolkit is not nearly as effective as a
  carpenter with a variety of tools.

- ▪ **How are results validated, tracked, and moved to the
  bottom line?** It is critical to establish a baseline for all ABM
  projects. Use financial staff to independently establish the baseline, verify the benefits, and drive the improvements to the bottom line by adjusting budgets and forecasts. The benefit
  validation should be within six months (preferably three
  months) of the ABM project implementation.

Establish an ABM Board and Process

If you ask a consultant to list critical success factors for any large
change initiative, the consultant will place Executive Sponsorship
at the top of the list. That's not to say that end-user buy-in is not
critical—it is. However, without strong executive sponsorship, any
enterprise-wide initiative, including ABM, will not realize its full
value . . . and may even completely fail.

A major component of an effective ABM program is the estab-
lishment of an ABM Board which, in essence, is an executive
steering committee. In order to demonstrate and cultivate strong
executive sponsorship, the ABM team should report monthly to an
ABM Board consisting of a cross-section of the top management
within the scope of the ABM initiative. In an enterprise-wide ABM
implementation, the ABM Board members should include the
heads of the major lines of business (LOBs), the head of operations
and either the corporate CFO or CEO.

The ultimate goal of the ABM Board is value realization—making decisions about ABM-related effort that result in shareholder value. The ABM Board objectives include:

- Create business value
- Align business and ABM strategies
- Ratify ABM budget goals and objectives
- Provide consistent ABM evaluations
- Generate ABM opportunities
- Communicate strategies, opportunities and results
- Commit and sponsor ABM projects

The ABM Board's actions are based on established ABM principles:

- Address important and contentious issues
- Clarify the company's position related to ABM
- Change behavior
- Collaborate across business lines
- Provide governance to ABM-related items
- Define the scope of ABM
- Drive ABM accountability
- Drive ABM communications and insight

The ABM team leader should prepare a monthly progress report for the ABM Board to communicate (1) current realized (signed-off) benefits, (2) the forecast of future benefits, (3) ABM project issues requiring the ABM Board's attention, and (4) a brief status of a few critical projects.

Figure 4.3 is a tried and true process for driving organizational change with an ABM Board. The process places a lot of responsibility in the hands of the ABM team (shown as Corp ABM Org). It is important to take a step-by-step walk-through of this critical process.

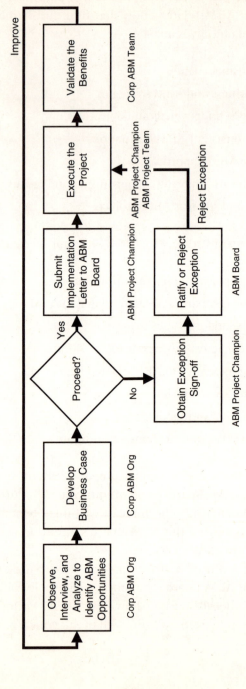

FIGURE 4.3 ABM Project Process with ABM Board

92

Observe, Interview, and Analyze to Identify ABM Opportunities

As shown in the first step, the ABM team is responsible for observing processes, interviewing employees, analyzing the ABC data to identify ABM opportunities. The attributes of the ABC model are extremely valuable in this step. The fixed/variable attributes and the Six Sigma attributes draw attention to significant savings through process improvement with immediate benefits. Also, the interviews cannot be understated. Interview the people doing the work and ask them the following:

- "What improvements would you like to see in your area?" This is an internally-focused question that emphasizes what the area can control. In many cases, the area has not had the time or resources to help Financial justify changes.

- "What changes in customer behavior (or technology) would most reduce your work?" This is an externally-focused question that emphasizes the cause-and-effect nature of ABC. Most of the time, this question leads to a wonderful brainstorming session. While many people are reluctant to discuss changes to their area, they are much less reluctant to discuss why other people need to change.

During this step, try to determine the appropriate ABM project champion. Who will drive the changes in the area? The project champion will own the results and, in the end, receive recognition from the ABM Board. The project champion is responsible for promoting and driving the project idea from conception through implementation and is often a mid-level manager or team leader.

Develop Business Case

It is important to have strong project financials skillsets on the ABM team. They need to translate the interviews, observations, and ABC data in the first step to cost-benefit analysis to develop the high-level business cases for potential ABM projects.

The business cases need to include the Net Income Before Taxes (NIBT) benefits due to revenue increases and expense reductions. Additionally, due to the risk emphasis in financial services, you may find it useful to break out risk reductions (such as fraud and operations losses) as a subset of expense reductions. A sample business case template is included on the companion website. Fortunately, as shown in the sample business template, most of the initial ABM projects will have payback periods of less than one year. With this in mind, the sample high-level business case focuses on costs and benefits of the first year.

Proceed?

Now you come to a decision point driven by the ABM team. Based on the shareholder value, ease of implementation, engagement of the project champion(s) and executive sponsor(s), risks of undertaking and not undertaking the project, and any other pertinent factors, does the ABM team recommend implementing this particular ABM project? Most of the time, the answer should be "yes" at this point.

Notice the ABM Board process is designed for a default answer of "yes." If the ABM team believes the ABM project is worth implementing, the burden of getting approval for *not* undertaking the project falls on the change obstructers and is represented by the project champion. This process is designed to overcome organizational inertia. Generally, the burden of proof is on the change agent (in this case, the ABM team). This process shifts the burden of proof to the potential change obstructers and, as you will see, the request not to implement the ABM project must be approved by the ABM Board.

Submit Implementation Letter to ABM Board

At this point, the ABM team and the project champion agree to implement the ABM project and there are no known obstructers. The Implementation Letter is a formal commitment from the project champion to deliver the ABM project. After discussing the ABM project and Implementation Letter with their executive sponsor (usually an ABM Board member), the project champion "sends" the Implementation Letter to the ABM Board. From a practical standpoint, the

Implementation Letter is not physically or electronically sent, but presented at the monthly ABM Board meeting.

A sample Implementation Letter is on the companion website. It includes a brief description of the project, the expected implementation date, and the expected implementation value.

Execute the Project

Of course, this is where the rubber meets the road: execution. The most effective ABM teams can fulfill many different roles at this step. For example, if the project champion and project team are extremely strong, the ABM team may only need to monitor progress through weekly status updates. However, if the project champion has weak project management skills, the ABM team needs to step up and either provides project management assistance or find project management assistance within the organization. Project management augmentation includes:

- Project planning
- Staffing
- Execution
- Communications
- Organizational change management
- Tracking

Similarly, if the project team does not have the required resources or availability to deliver the project, the ABM team should assist by either providing resources or helping to procure resources.

Validate the Benefits

After the ABM benefits have reached steady state (or can be clearly forecast), it is important to validate the benefits. This means that Finance personnel must independently confirm the benefits and incorporate these benefits into ongoing forecasts and budgets. This is the only way to maintain the financial integrity of the ABM efforts. A finance resource should be assigned to the ABM team to quantify the results of each ABM project and determine the value by LOB.

Next, the ABM Finance resource needs to review the results with each line of business CFO impacted by the ABM project and obtain sign-off. The CFO sign-off indicates the CFO team has incorporated the validated ABM benefits into ongoing forecasts and budgets.

Also, to avoid confusion, the ABM finance resources needs to review the ABM project pipeline with each line of business CFO during the annual budget cycle to ensure that a consistent proba- bility-weighted amount of ABM benefits is incorporated in LOB budgets. For example, if the ABM finance resource estimates ten future ABM projects to be worth $20 million in the upcoming fiscal year, with a 75% likelihood of realizing this value, the LOB budgets need to reflect $15 million of ABM improvements. Only variances from this budget require forecast adjustments.

Obtain Exception Sign-Off

Now let's discuss the exception process. As mentioned above, the exception process places the burden of proof on the obstructer. For a legitimate exception to occur, the ABM team and the potential ABM project champion (or a powerful stakeholder) must disagree on the holistic impact to the bottom line. This is quite rare. In my experience using this process, the ratio of implemented projects to projects granted an exception is approximately 50 to 1. That said, this successful ratio is highly dependent upon the ABM team's approach.

Prior to making it to the decision point and certainly before going down the exception path, the ABM team needs to establish buy-in in the areas impacted by the ABM project. Identify all stakeholders and understand their needs and concerns. If necessary, have the opposing group document all their concerns and document all mitigations to those concerns. For some concerns, there may be no mitigating actions, but at least the issues are identified and documented. Always remember that ABM improvements should be done *with* the impacted areas . . . not *to* the impacted areas!

An exception request template is included on the companion website and should include the following sections to be completed by the exception requestor:

- Exception Justification
- Estimated Value of the Exception
- Other Quantification of the Exception (such as quantified customer attrition, employee turnover, new names, etc.)
- Qualified Value of Exception (such as reputational risk, etc.)
- What conditions would need to change before implementing this recommendation?

The requestor's answer to the last question is extremely telling. If the requestor does not believe that the ABM project is worthwhile under any circumstances (or "When pigs fly!"), it is pretty clear that you have a bigger issue on your hand. Assuming that you have a competent ABM team, there should always be conditions when it is appropriate to implement the ABM improvement. The question prompts the requestor to become part of the solution by identifying the "right" conditions for the ABM improvement.

Ratify or Reject the Exception

Ultimately, in this process neither the ABM team nor the person requesting the exception has the final say. The exception request should be presented by the exception requestor to the ABM Board as part of the monthly meeting. As the leader of the ABM team, you will need to present the facts regarding the benefits of the ABM project. In essence, this is the exception request's "day in court." Since there should be no court of appeal, you and your team need to be comfortable with the decision of the ABM Board.

Before you undertake the ABC/M project, have a realistic understanding with the project sponsor regarding the ABM Board. Determine if you are being asked to be the captain of the Titanic *before* you accept the position. Frankly, if the commitment does not exist to have regular open dialog and accountability with the ABM Board, do not accept the ABC/M assignment—you have an iceberg in your way.

Track ABM Progress versus the Baseline

Throughout this book, the importance of establishing baselines is emphasized several times. If you do not really know where you started on the journey, how do you measure progress?

For individual ABM projects, remember to normalize baselines. Normalization is division of data by a common variable in order to allow for comparability on common scale. For example, the phrase "Six Sigma" was based on the number of defects per million opportunities which is a form of normalization (x per y). If Insurance Agent Albert creates three new policy errors per month and Insurance Agent Betty creates ten new policy errors per month, you may believe that Betty's process produces lower quality results. However, if Albert generates only three new policies per month and Betty generates two hundred, clearly Albert has the lower quality process.

Similarly, if you are trying to improve Accounts Receivable (A/R), look at the days' sales outstanding (DSO or days' receivables), not the absolute dollars in A/R. Days' sales outstanding is the ratio of A/R to Sales for the period. As the company grows, so will A/R (ceteris paribus). Therefore, the normalized ratio of days' sales outstanding is a better baseline and monitoring measurement.

For the entire ABM project portfolio, the ABM progress versus the baseline shown in terms of NIBT should be communicated to the ABM Board on a monthly basis. An example of the NIBT progress versus the baseline is shown in Figure 4.4.

Celebrate Successes and Milestones

Now comes the fun part: the celebrations and rewards!! This is extremely important to the long-term success of the ABM initiative, team and you. Make certain to cast the net wide for recognitions, but also differentiate some of the rewards. Here are a few ideas:

- Take anyone involved in the ABM success to a ballgame when the project reaches the $5 or $10 million milestone. It is amazing how often corporate-sponsored loges sit empty because

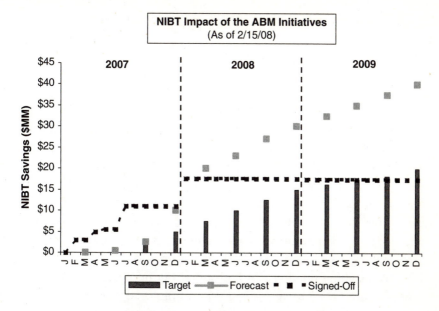

FIGURE 4.4 Monthly NIBT Impact of ABM Projects

companies cannot find clients willing to be entertained every night. Use one of these nights for your team. If they achieved $5 million of NIBT improvements in one year, they are providing more value than most of your customers!

- Nominate the highest value teams for a corporate recognition.
- Give the team members an extra week of vacation.
- Award weekend getaways for the families.
- Publish the successes in the corporate newsletter or on the corporate website.
- Encourage team members and key contributors to present their results at internal and external events. Publicly demonstrating the success of the team also helps to recruit talent to the team and the company.

Bottom line: You should know what makes your team "tick" and fulfill the need to be recognized for a job well done. Make certain that the praise and rewards are sincere.

DIFFERENCES BETWEEN ABM AND ABC STAFFING

One major difference between ABM and ABC implementations is the make-up of the staff. Typically, many of the resources of an ABC implementation have accounting and financial systems backgrounds. Workstreams of an ABC project plan are fairly common: costing policy and design, activity and driver interviews, model build and technology, driver collection and technology, and reporting and technology. If a few of the team leaders have implemented ABC in the past, the project plan is fairly clear at the project kick-off. Unfortunately, the ABC team might not include any Product Management experience on the team and while this team might not negatively impact the delivery of ABC, the odds of a successful ABM implementation are much lower if the ABC staffing is maintained, as is, throughout ABM implementation.

ABM staffing requires three attributes not needed in the ABC implementation: (1) a broader business experience and sense of ownership, (2) an ability and comfort creating definition in the face of ambiguity, and (3) project leadership with project portfolio management experience. A word of caution: Just because the skills required vary between ABC and ABM implementations does not mean that the entire ABC team should be swapped out for the new ABM team. Hopefully, the ABC team was staffed with ABM in mind (begin with the end in mind) and at least 30% of the resources can be used for ABM. Otherwise, you will lose important continuity and knowledge required for successful ABM implementation.

Business Experience and Sense of Ownership

The more knowledgeable the ABM team is from a financial, process, project, and political standpoint, the greater the likelihood of success. It is most effective to recommend lLOB representation to each of the executives on the ABM Board. For example, in the insurance industry, request that the heads of products for Property and Casualty, Individual Life, and Institutional Life be single points of contact and direct extensions of the core ABM team. Hopefully, the ABC team worked directly with these individuals to help design the ABC/M system. They should be some of your most active and visible supporters of ABC/M.

These imbedded ABC/M resources act as "tentacles" for the core ABM team. They feel the pulse of their organization, know what approaches work in their areas, and have the respect and political power within their organizations to drive change. It is essential to recognize these individuals as leaders on the ABM team. As the ABM team reaches critical milestones and recognitions, these individuals should be recognized and should assist in the recognition of others within their organizations.

Definition in the Face of Ambiguity

One of the greatest intangible skills required of the ABM team will be the reduction of ambiguity. Taking a gray cloud situation and making it black and white requires a very structured and logical approach and thought process. Look to staff ABM resources that have a track record of taking nebulous situations and clearing them up ("We seem to be losing customers to John Hancock. If this is true, go figure out why and reverse the trend,""Something just isn't right in Branches. Look into it and fix it," or "We want you to implement Six Sigma in Operations"). To accomplish these types of objectives, the ABM resources need a great ability to learn quickly, structured thinking and leadership abilities.

PROJECT PORTFOLIO MANAGEMENT

From an ABC/M team leadership perspective, the shift from ABC to ABM is quite dramatic, too. The ABC team had common, well-documented goals regarding the successful on-time delivery of the ABC system. On the other hand, the ABM team has a continual broad goal: maximize long-term shareholder value by increasing NIBT through the use of ABC information to improve overall performance. There is not a single point in time for delivery. There is no longer a single project. ABM is a portfolio of projects and should be managed as such.

From the Project Management Institute's *PMBOK® Guide*[1]:

> Portfolio: A collection of projects or programs and other work that are grouped together to facilitate effective management of that work to meet strategic business objectives.

(Project) Portfolio Management: The centralized management of one or more portfolios which includes identifying, prioritizing, authorizing, managing and controlling projects, programs and other related work to achieve specific business objectives.

Project Portfolio Management Tools and Techniques

Several tools and techniques can be used to help prioritize the ABM project portfolio. In the early stages of ABM, use the simplest tools because there is a lot of low-hanging fruit and trying to finely cut the projects at this stage using more sophisticated methods and tools is overkill.

Two-by-Two Implementation/Benefit Matrix

As shown earlier in Figure 4.1, the two-by-two Implementation/ Benefit Matrix is a simple, yet effective, method of separating the ABM projects into four distinct quadrants. It really is effective in separating the proverbial wheat from the chaff. It is not particularly helpful in a more granular cut that may be necessary to resolve resource, risk, or timing constraints. Using this tool early in the ABM process requires the ABM team leader to make the finer cut.

Pair-Wise Ranking

Pair-wise ranking can be one of the simplest methods of project ranking. Pair-wise is usually performed on a portfolio of projects between ten and fifty. As its name implies, pair-wise ranking compares each individual project to every other individual project to determine the "winner." Think of it as a round-robin tournament between all of the projects in a portfolio.

Figure 4.5 shows a sample result of a pair-wise ranking for Projects A–G. The comparison is usually not based on a single quantified criterion or rigid scoring. It is generally based on a hard criterion (such as NIBT value) augmented by the team's qualified assessment of the

Project vs.	Project					
	B	C	D	E	F	G
A	B	C	A	A	F	A
B		C	B	B	F	B
C			C	C	C	C
D				D	F	D
E					F	G
F						F

FIGURE 4.5 Sample Pair-Wise Ranking Results

likelihood and speed of success which incorporates attributes such as implementation risk, sponsorship, and organizational readiness.

The winner of the pair-wise round-robin tournament in Figure 4.5 is Project C. When compared on an individual basis, Project C was better than every project. The second highest priority project is Project F which had five wins and so on down to Project E which had no wins.

Balanced Scorecard Ranking

The Balanced Scorecard Ranking approach is based on Kaplan and Norton's balanced scorecard work. Depending on your organization's level of sophistication, buy-in, and use of balanced scorecards, this tool may be useful in structuring the ABM project portfolio. However, if the balanced scorecard is not already widely used within your organization, I do not recommend prioritizing your ABM projects using this method. You will already have enough organizational change efforts to instill ABM within the organization. Even though the balanced scorecard can be extremely valuable, introducing it via the ABM project is too much for any ABM team to handle.

For those organizations using the balanced scorecard, aligning the projects to the scorecard can be a great prioritization and communication tool. The ranking simply involves aligning the projects to the scorecard as shown in Figure 4.6. The concept is to ensure the ABM project portfolio contains projects that address each of the perspectives—Financial, Customer, Internal Business Processes, and Innovation and Learning—to enable the organization's vision and strategy.

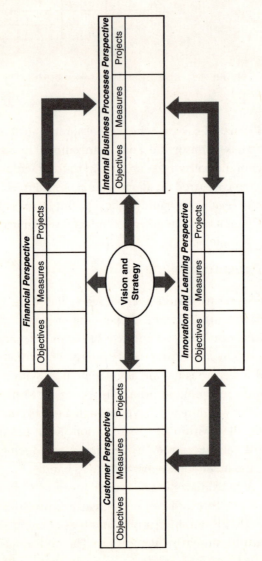

FIGURE 4.6 Balanced Scorecard Project Ranking

Portfolio Ranking Tool

The most quantified approach to project prioritization is a portfolio ranking tool. This type of project prioritization is especially useful when the portfolio size becomes greater than fifty and resources are very limited. All projects are given a total score based on pre-established standard criteria and weighting. The example shown in Figure 4.7 demonstrates a portfolio ranked on only four criteria—strategic alignment, shareholder value (NIBT), implementation risk, and duration. Based on the total results, Project B is the highest priority and Project D is the lowest priority.

The scoring criteria should be well-defined. For instance, a High score on Strategic Alignment should be the result of the project being explicitly identified in the corporation's strategic plan while a Medium score is a potential enabler to the strategic plan and not explicitly identified in the plan. It is important to set the criteria prior to ranking the projects for the first time. Otherwise, there can be a lot of gamesmanship to change the criteria to match the preconceived desired prioritization.

Portfolio ranking tools will be as simple or complex as you allow them to be. For example, is Net Shareholder Value (NIBT) simply based on the Net Present Value (NPV) of the project? Or is it based on the Economic Value Added (EVA)? Or is it based on a combination of EVA and payback period?

If you decide to use a portfolio ranking tool, I recommend that you keep the criteria small and simple. Use the tool for guidance, not absolute results. By "guidance," I mean that the tool will identify three classes of projects during the prioritization: clear high priority projects that need your team's attention and will be staffed, clear low priority projects that do not need your team's attention and will not be staffed, and projects that fall in between. How you manage and staff these "in between" projects will require your focus. Whether or not you implement these projects will depend on many factors ranging from corporate and global economic conditions to your individual political influence. Your judgment, not a rigid scoring tool, will be the key to your success.

| Project | Strategic Alignment | | | Net Shareholder Value (EBIT) | | | Implementation Risk | | | Project Duration | | | Total Results |
	High = 10 Med = 5 Low = 1	Weight	Subtotal	High = 10 Med = 5 Low = 1	Weight	Subtotal	High = 1 Med = 5 Low = 10	Weight	Subtotal	Long = 1 Med = 5 Short = 10	Weight	Subtotal	
Project A	5	10	50	5	10	50	10	7	70	1	3	3	173
Project B	10	10	100	5	10	50	5	7	35	5	3	15	200
Project C	1	10	10	10	10	100	1	7	7	5	3	15	132
Project D	5	10	50	1	10	10	5	7	35	10	3	30	125

FIGURE 4.7 Project Portfolio Ranking Tool Example

DRIVING RESULTS

So far, this book has laid out a lot of tangible steps and deliverables to assist with ABC/M implementation. This section is focused on several additional considerations you will encounter while driving ABM benefits to the bottom line.

Align Business and ABM Strategies

What keeps the CEO up at night? That is a fundamental question in a consultant's repertoire. It is not a trick question. It is a question that forces you to examine how much your ABM projects directly or indirectly address the CEO's concerns. In all likelihood, the CEO is concerned with the execution of the corporate strategy and/or current operational issues. How do your ABC/M projects address these concerns?

If the corporate strategy is centered on the customer experience and the ABM projects are saving costs with a side-effect of deteriorating the customer experience, you have got a problem on your hands. You would be better off using ABM to map the customer experience and eliminate low quality and NVA work. Make sure you anticipate the full-picture impact of the ABM changes before implementing the projects. The full-picture impact includes alignment to the business strategy.

Chapter 6 contains a broader discussion of organizational alignment and organizational change management considerations and tools.

Align Control and Accountability

The number one common obstacle to change is the misalignment between control and accountability, including goal misalignment. Goal misalignment includes the sales personnel compensated based on revenue, not profit: the branch manager that controls cash levels, but does not have the carrying cost of cash on his or her income statement and the IT project manager that is rewarded for "on time, on budget," but not for becoming more efficient through code reuse or other methods. Find and fix these types of problems as often as you can.

In one particular case, we discovered a customer driving up inventory levels because the sales personnel (compensation based on revenue) agreed to an order lead time that was shorter than our lead time with our supplier. Excluding the carrying cost of the inventory, the profit margin was already razor thin, but that did not really matter to the sales team. With the customer's high volume, the sales team made a tidy commission based solely on the revenue. However, the company's shareholders were losing hundreds of thousands of dollars each month due to the deal. Unfortunately, this was not easily observed in the previous non-ABC cost allocation method. The inventory carrying costs were spread among a variety of customers and, worse yet, among products that had nothing to do with the inventory. Due to inaccurate costing, both the customer relationship and the product appeared profitable, but, in fact, both were hemorrhaging shareholder value. Ouch!

When asked what this deal would do the company's inventory, the sales person responded, "It will put the inventory through the roof . . . but that's not my concern. They pay me to sell." That person is selling at another company now and the contract was restructured with the customer to allow for a fair value exchange.

If you consider the past several years in financial services, the damage that can be done by misalignment of control and accountability is vividly apparent. Mortgage brokers were paid to sell mortgages without any accountability for the quality of the mortgages (defaults). In the beginning of the mortgage cycle, commercial banks were also not accountable for the quality of the mortgages, since they were packaged and sold as individual mortgages to Fannie and Freddie or collateralized and sold as bonds. Either way, the commercial banks were left carrying only a small percentage of the mortgages. Later, of course, this "small percentage" of toxic loans grew to become a meaningful portion of the banks' balance sheets. However, did a mortgage broker's commission ever suffer as a result of these defaults? No. The accountability had traditionally been with the commercial banks as the holders of the mortgages. But, as commercial banks sold the mortgages, more risk was shifted from the commercial banks to the bond holders. Unfortunately, most banks underestimated their remaining exposure in this new world.

Establish ABM Budget, Forecast, and Actual Results

One version of tracking ABM projects to a baseline is tracking ABM actual results to the budget and forecast. Figure 4.8 provides an example of a simple tracking report.

The annual ABM budget NIBT savings needs to be developed for each ABM project and incorporated into the budgets of the various LOBs impacted. Closing the loop by including validated benefits in the budget assists in driving ABM results. If the benefits are in the budget, the LOBs will more actively support the efforts to implement the changes. Figure 4.8 is a summary of the monthly tracking tool used at the monthly ABM Board meetings.

Improve Processes

ABM projects will likely fall into two main types of projects: process/policy improvement and consumption improvement (specifically, unprofitable customers and/or behaviors). Several techniques can be used for process improvement projects including Six Sigma's DMAIC, TQM, and workout sessions.

Create the appropriate baseline data based on resource utilization, cycle time, and quality. Determine how to measure the improvement in terms of a NIBT impact. To remain truly focused on the bottom line,

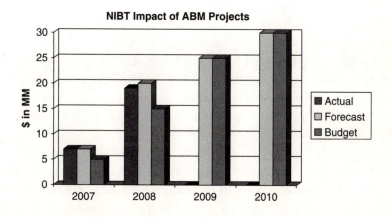

FIGURE 4.8 ABM Budget, Forecast, and Actual Results

value cost avoidance, and employee and customer satisfaction as $0 NIBT. While there is value in both employee and customer satisfaction, unless these numbers are converted into employee/customer attrition and a hard dollar NIBT with an associated cost center and account, it is better to spend your efforts on more certain value. I have seen too many value-destroying pet projects labeled "employee satisfaction" and I am jaded. Once, during a due diligence meeting, the IT lead commented that every one of the claims operators needed their own desktop personal computer rather than the old "dumb" terminals they currently used. Their throughput on the dumb terminals was significantly above the industry average and higher than the acquiring company, so I asked why they needed the PCs. "To improve employee morale by providing them with e-mail capabilities," she answered. Oh, I thought they were there to process claims. I wonder what their throughput is now . . .

Improve Consumption

Many people stop ABM at the process improvement level, but improving unprofitable customers, products and behaviors can be extremely valuable. Figure 4.9 is the re-introduction of the Cliff Chart from Chapter 1. Remember, this Cliff Chart represents that the median customer is the breakeven customer with a maximum cumulative profit of $466 million. $190 million of value is destroyed by relationships with customers to the right of the midpoint.

So, what do we do with those pesky unprofitable customers? Divest them? Well, in the case of the increased inventory levels driven by sales personnel lead time agreements, four of the top ten product users had unprofitable relationships with the company. While the other three relationships did not destroy value on the "hundreds of thousands of dollars" level, each remediation used the following process:

1. Carefully examine the entire relationship including the fixed and variable impacts of the customer divesture. Examine any dependencies between the customer and other customers. Brainstorm solutions controlled by your company, such as

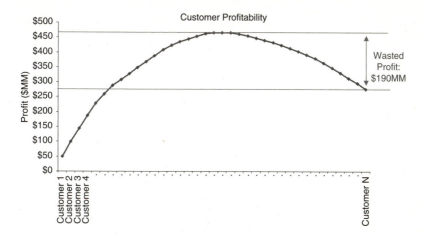

FIGURE 4.9 Customer Cliff Chart

process improvements, and solutions controlled by the customer, such as customer lead times.

2. Once you are comfortable with the facts, sit down with the customer to explain your position and the alternatives. Generally, by the time you meet with the customer, you should have already implemented or committed to implement every known non-customer-impacting improvement. Present several alternatives for the customer and work with them to determine the pros and cons of each solution from their perspective.

3. In some cases, it may be evident that it is not in your shareholders' long-term best interest to maintain the business without major customer behavioral changes. If the customer is not willing to make those changes, assist the customer in moving their business to your competitor.

In most cases, the solution will be a combination of customer behavior changes and price increases. The value exchange of the product and the price was beneficial to both shareholder groups. The process listed above is reinforced in "The Right Way to Manage Unprofitable Customers."[2]

Sometimes, it is necessary to realize some lost customers are "addition by subtraction." As a Cleveland resident for nearly fifteen years, I am frequently reminded of the Cleveland-based Progressive Insurance model of customer selection. Because Progressive Insurance is so confident in their modeling of the expected profit of each individual relationship, they show the quotes of other insurance companies on the Progressive website. Basically, if another insurance provider will charge less than Progressive, Progressive would like you to go to the competition. In essence, Progressive is confident the competition will not get an acceptable profit margin from the relationship. Progressive benefits in two ways: (1) higher profit margins for Progressive, and (2) lower profit margins for their competition.

The driving force for making customer relationships profitable is very simple: As an employee, you have a fiduciary responsibility to your shareholders to make a fair value exchange which includes a profit. Meanwhile, in many cases, corporations will pound the table year after year saying, "We need to drive more sales. We need more customers!" In actuality, sometimes what they really need is to make the customers they already have more profitable.

Leverage the Predictive Power of ABC

Because of the power of the attributes that you incorporated when you built the ABC model, it has tremendous predictive capability. Specifically, the fixed and variable attributes used in the resource module help to identify the impacts from customer behavioral shifts. You can examine this information on a customer-by-customer basis which will be invaluable for corporate/institutional relationships, and on a channel or product basis for retail analysis. Let's look at an example.

Prior to implementing ABC, most companies look at the average profitability of products and relationships. Within these averages there is a lot of opportunity for improvement. Figure 4.10 represents two retail customers with the same single product. They both initiated seventeen transactions during the month. Prior to ABC, they were probably viewed as equally profitable. However, after implementing ABC and differentiating the channel costs, it can be seen that Customer B's heavy reliance on branch transactions make him roughly ten times more costly to serve.

If these two customers were corporate or institutional customers, the cost differences would be orders of magnitude higher and could be

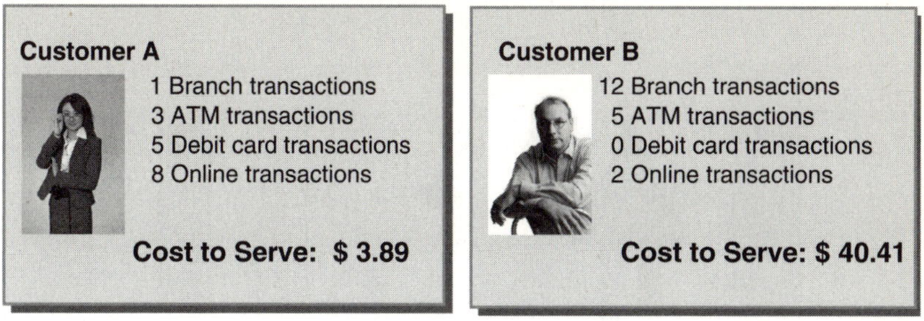

Customer A

1 Branch transactions
3 ATM transactions
5 Debit card transactions
8 Online transactions

Cost to Serve: $ 3.89

Customer B

12 Branch transactions
5 ATM transactions
0 Debit card transactions
2 Online transactions

Cost to Serve: $ 40.41

FIGURE 4.10 Customer Cost to Serve Differences by Channel

addressed on an individual basis. However, since we are talking about a difference of only $36 per month, who really cares, right?

Figure 4.11 shows why we should care. It uses the predictive nature of the ABC results to show that a customer-wide shift from branch transactions to ATM transactions has large potential value. A 25% shift from branch to ATM will result in nearly $500,000 in benefit. As the ABM projects are identified, use the predictive information (fixed/variable and cost of quality attributes) to help identify and quantify improvement opportunities.

ADDITIONAL CONSIDERATIONS FOR FINANCIAL SERVICES

Implementing ABC/M at any corporation involves industry-specific considerations and the financial services industry is no exception. The additional considerations for financial services include industry differences due to all three potential system components: people, process, and technology.

Financial Acumen: Friend and Foe

From a personnel standpoint, the financial services industry is loaded with people well versed in specific areas of accounting and finance including traditional accounting, budgeting and forecasting, actuarial analysis, balance sheet management, treasury management, mergers and acquisitions, derivatives, equity and bond fund management, funds transfer pricing, and capital allocation—just to name a few.

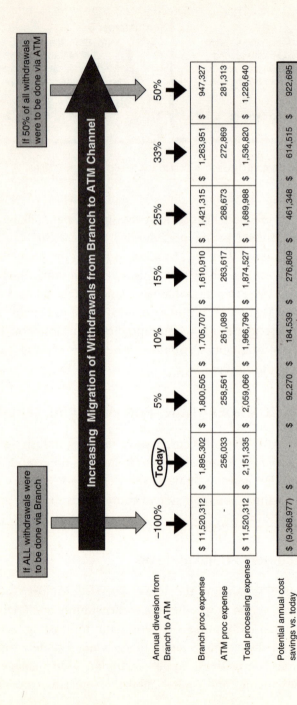

If ALL withdrawals were to be done via Branch

If 50% of all withdrawals were to be done via ATM

Increasing Migration of Withdrawals from Branch to ATM Channel

	−100%	Today	5%	10%	15%	25%	33%	50%
Annual diversion from Branch to ATM								
Branch proc expense	$ 11,520,312	$ 1,895,302	$ 1,800,505	$ 1,705,707	$ 1,610,910	$ 1,421,315	$ 1,263,951	$ 947,327
ATM proc expense	-	256,033	258,561	261,089	263,617	268,673	272,869	281,313
Total processing expense	$ 11,520,312	$ 2,151,335	$ 2,059,066	$ 1,966,796	$ 1,874,527	$ 1,689,988	$ 1,536,820	$ 1,228,640
Potential annual cost savings vs. today	$ (9,368,977)	$ -	$ 92,270	$ 184,539	$ 276,809	$ 461,348	$ 614,515	$ 922,695

FIGURE 4.11 Predictive Costing Provides Information to Encourage Channel Migration

Clearly, this can be an advantage from a communication and understanding standpoint.

However, the other side of this double-edged sword is painful. Because of the sheer number of people with specialized financial knowledge within financial services, you will encounter more people who believe they have a deep knowledge of costing and, more specifically, ABC. In my years of experience, there are many more people that *think* they know ABC than actually do.

ABC/M is a specialty and while it can be understood in a matter of hours, just like any of the financial specialties mentioned above, it takes years of real experience to grasp, design, and implement the nuances and subtleties required to make a world-class ABC/M program. Implementing ABC/M within financial services takes additional patience to educate some of the existing "experts" who have never implemented an ABC/M program.

Cost Allocations Outside of ABC

Unlike many industries, financial services products have very few direct material costs. The sales component within financial services is large, but the transaction processing costs are reduced on a daily basis. Within banking, in particular, the ABC system typically does not even contain two significant sources of funding costs: Funds Transfer Pricing (FTP) and capital (equity) charges. In many cases, these two sources of costs drive behavior more than the ABC model and need to be briefly discussed.

Funds Transfer Pricing

Banking 101 taught us that banks need to duration match their assets (loans and other funding uses) and liabilities (deposits and other funding sources). Therefore, banks need to determine the duration of each of the products to determine the correct matching. This can be accomplished through estimates of industry averages which provide a very general answer for each product, or through heavy statistical analysis associated with static pool modeling, the discussion of which is beyond the scope of this book. Once the durations are known, the balance sheet can be more effectively matched and managed.

That left banking with another perplexing question from an incentive and recognition standpoint: If we fund an 8% loan with a 2% deposit, how should the 6% spread benefit be split between the loan and the deposit? What was the incremental spread value of the loan? What was the incremental spread value of the deposit?

The answers to these questions are provided by the bank's FTP system. In its most simplistic form the FTP curve can set to be the London Interbank Offered Rate (LIBOR) curve since this represents interbank borrowing rates. Loans and deposits can be compared against the FTP rates to determine expected incremental value.

For instance, if a consumer buys a $10,000 one-year certificate of deposit (CD) with a 2% yield, the product is compared to the FTP (LIBOR in this example). If the one-year LIBOR is 4.5%, the incremental funding benefit of the deposit is $250 ($10,000 at 2.5%). The bank will pay 2% on the deposit and can make 4.5% via the interbank market without making an additional loan.

Conversely, using the same LIBOR curve, if a consumer takes out a $10,000 one-year term loan with an 8% interest rate, the incremental interest benefit to the bank is $350 ($10,000 at 3.5%). The bank will receive 8% interest will borrowing at the 4.5% LIBOR rate.

But what does this have to do with costing? Well, the FTP cost associated with the loan is viewed as a 4.5% charge. Given the potential magnitude of these FTP charges, it may not be possible to get the attention of lending lines of business using ABC if they believe the FTP charges are unduly inaccurate.

So, while it is possible to increase the accuracy of the FTP charges by using a curve more reflective of the particular bank's available external funding sources and implemented deposit and credit liquidity premiums, it may cause unforeseen distractions from the ABM improvements. In any case, strong and clear FTP policies are extremely helpful to the ABM effort.

Capital Charges[3]

Similar to FTP, banks allocate (not assign) capital to assets to ensure for adequate coverage in the event of losses. The cost of capital is also allocated to these assets.

Generally, capital is allocated on a risk-adjusted basis with the riskiest assets requiring the highest percentage of capital. For example, some government securities and cash are considered risk-free and required no capital allocation while many loans require an 8% capital allocation.

Once again, the issue for ABM implementation is one of focus. If the capital charge policies are strong and clear, the lending lines of business are more able to focus on process and customer improvements using ABM.

Information Technology Costs

Due to the nature of the industry, IT costs within financial services continue to replace direct material and physical handling costs. Currency and coin usage has been declining at roughly 5% per year for many years. Even though checks will continue to be used for decades, physical handling of checks has been virtually eliminated with the passage of Check 21.[4]

Because of the higher percentage of IT costs within financial services, it is essential that the ABC system integrate and accurately convey the IT costs as they supplant the Front Office and Operations costs. Ignoring or using broad-brush allocation techniques for IT costs is unacceptable within financial services. Specific techniques for assigning IT costs to products and customers will be discussed in Chapter 5.

Data, Data Everywhere

A man with one watch always knows the time. A man with two watches is never sure.

—Unknown

No collection of industries has more information about you and your family than financial services. Insurance companies know information about you and your family's doctors, illnesses, cures, frequency of visits, and number of real teeth (believe me . . . I worked on an insurance claims conversion project). And unless you use cash for all of your purchases, banks know your income, frequency of deposits, mortgage payments, magazine subscriptions, travel destinations, favorite restaurants, make and model of your car, all your online purchases, and alimony or child support payments. Kind of scary, huh? Of course, I can't help wondering, if the bank knows so much about me, why do I continually have to select English at the ATM when I have pushed the same button for five years? One day, I just want to insert my ATM card and see, "Welcome back, Brent! Same as last time ($100)?" One button—done.

The financial service industry is clearly awash in data. On one hand, this is good for ABC/M implementations. You should be able to find an automated source for most of your driver data.

On the other hand, inconsistent data on the same topic is painful and the financial services industry is full of it. Inconsistent data analysis exists for several reasons including:

- **Availability of the source data.** Some data pulls are intentionally designed to provide directional snapshots before the data is final. These situations should be understood and communicated.

- **Pulling obsolete data.** Some data analysis tools pull from sources that were replaced and are now obsolete. These situations need to be corrected.

- **Some data analysis is predictive ("what if").** Just as forecast and actual data differ, any predictive system will vary from actual results. A salesperson once questioned why the sales estimation tool was always slightly different from the true account profitability. Slight variances should always be expected in this case.

- **Difference in methodology.** In one case, we uncovered a data analyst using "industry standard" costs for profitability reporting instead of the product costs provided by ABC. This type of reporting was not helpful in making the right business decisions and was replaced by consistent ABC information.

In the end, the amount of data within financial services can be a blessing and curse. Be prepared to understand and act on the variety of data. "Data, data everywhere, but not a drop to drink" can sometimes feel like the Rhyme of the Ancient ABCer in financial services.

NOTES

1. *PMBOK® Guide*, Project Management Institute, Inc., Newtown Square, PA, 2000.
2. *The Right Way to Manage Unprofitable Customers*, Vikas Mittal, Matthew Sarkees, and Feisal Murshed, *Harvard Business Review*, April 2008.
3. For a comprehensive insight into bank capital management, read *Managing Bank Capital: Capital Allocation and Performance Measurement* by Chris Matten. (West Sussex, UK: John Wiley & Sons, 2000).
4. "The Check Clearing for the 21st Century Act (Check 21) was signed into law on October 28, 2003, and became effective on October 28, 2004. Check 21 is designed to foster innovation in the payments system and to enhance its efficiency by reducing some of the legal impediments to check truncation. The law facilitates check truncation by creating a new negotiable instrument called a substitute check, which permits banks to truncate original checks, to process check information electronically, and to deliver substitute checks to banks that want to continue receiving paper checks. A substitute check is the legal equivalent of the original check and includes all the information contained on the original check. The law does not require banks to accept checks in electronic form nor does it require banks to use the new authority granted by the Act to create substitute checks." (Source: www.federalreserve.gov/paymentsystems/truncation/).

CHAPTER 5

ABC/M in Shared Services

Beware of the man who won't be bothered with details.

—William Feather

STARTING ABC/M WITH SHARED SERVICES

Since two of the primary reasons for implementing activity-based costing are understanding and, hopefully, improving indirect costs such as those previously allocated from Operations, Information Technology (IT), Human Resources (HR) and Finance, these shared services are common starting points for ABC/M implementation. Within the financial services industry, in particular, IT and Operations are the most common starting points due to their relatively high expenses.

Additionally, there are two common complaints about the IT costs from the lines of business (LOBs):

1. **"I don't understand our IT costs"** This claim sometimes has two very legitimate components—a lack of transparency which should be the first priority of the ABC implementation and a lack of a common language which will be discussed shortly.

2. **"The IT costs are too high"** This complaint always perplexes me. If the LOBs do not understand the IT costs, how can they

claim the costs are too high? Ask for a benchmark or other indicator that the IT costs are "too high." Certainly, IT costs have been growing for the past several decades. However, these costs provide scalability and reduce costs in the front office. Of course, the IT costs are growing while the Front Office or Operations costs are shrinking— these comments are two sides of the same coin. However, the increases in IT costs should be improving the overall efficiency. In banking, for example, investments in technology should be improving the efficiency ratio.

To be clear, I am not putting IT on a pedestal and saying that there is never any room for improvement within the area. There is room for improvement within any organization. Studies from PMI (Project Management Institute) and SEI (Software Engineering Institute) repeatedly show that most IT organizations have opportunities for improvement. However, we need to deal with facts, not hearsay. It should be culturally unacceptable to say, "Organization X's costs are too high" without the facts to back up the statement.

COMMUNICATION BARRIERS

"The moose is loose!" meant that the power/thermal subsystem on the mainframe computer was up and running. Well, that was according to one of the highest technical resources within IBM's mainframe hardware division. The communication was not jargon, but it certainly was not clear to the uninitiated. If you want to speak in code, immerse yourself in any specialty and become a specialist.

The front office, by its customer-facing nature, needs to be somewhat of a generalist—able to address a variety of customer needs and multiple product inquiries. The back office (shared services) contains many more specialists. At times, the communication between generalists and specialists can create a type of communication barrier within an organization. ABC has a tendency to uncover these differences and, at times, become a translational tool to help the generalists understand the specialists.

Translating Operations Activities

Due to the emphasis on process and staffing within bank operations, "Deposit a check" in a traditional paper check environment is broken down into a lot of activities including encoding (proof), first-pass capture, group sort, fine sort, reject repair, cash letter preparation, local clearing, nonlocal clearing, and settlement. The Operations group needs to manage these activities, but the LOB is not usually interested in the detail. This where the activity hierarchy recommended in Chapter 3 becomes particularly useful. The ABC model can be used to provide the detail required by bank operations, provide the summary required by the LOB, and provide visual translation and transparency to overcome the communication barrier.

Another consideration of Operations activities is that the LOB, product and customer attributes that were so well defined in the front office are intentionally homogeneous in the shared services environment. The check-encoding area does not have dedicated units for savings deposits, corporate deposits, and personal deposits for each LOB. It is all one unit. By design, shared services are most effective if there are minimal LOB-specific or product-specific instructions. Therefore, it is particularly important to track account numbers for all costs to be assigned to specific customers and products.

Translating IT Applications

Translating IT applications to meaningful activities can be a bit of a sticky wicket. To understand and improve the application costs, the IT shared services organization typically will use ABC to assign the costs to support storage, the processing (either measured in Millions of Instructions Per Second (MIPS) or Central Processing Unit (CPU) seconds, or a portion of a shared server), other peripheral devices and human support. Added to the direct license and maintenance charges for each application, these assigned costs provide a reasonably accurate cost of each application. Since the applications are typically cost objects in the IT shared services ABC model, from an IT standpoint, the ABC/M system is sometimes viewed as complete.

Clearly, though, the costs have not been assigned to products or customers. The applications (cost objects) of the IT ABC model are actually the resources for the other areas of the organization. In this way, IT application costs require a two-step integrated approach for driving costs to customers. Three different methods for accomplishing this model integration are highlighted at the end of this chapter.

EXPECTED DIALOG FOR PLANNING

As a company moves forward with predictive ABC using either strict activity-based budgeting (ABB) or driver-based budgeting as a guide, there must be an established, straightforward dialog between the shared service areas and the LOBs regarding the drivers.

For example, in order to develop an accurate staffing and expense plan, bank operations needs to know the following:

- The number of checks to be processed
- The number of automated clearing house (ACH) debits to be processed
- The number of ACH credits to be processed
- The number of manual statements to be generated and sent
- The number of Non-Sufficient Funds (NSF) notifications to be generated and sent

But here is the disconnect: It is not realistic to ask Retail Product Management to plan to this level. Retail Product Management is focused on numbers of accounts and value of those accounts (deposit or loan volume). In such case, Retail should focus its planning efforts on something we will discuss next: master drivers.

Master Drivers for Retail or Individual Accounts

Master drivers are the essential, large-volume business drivers that cause a predictable movement in many underlying drivers. Figure 5.1 provides a simplified example of the historical relationship between three master drivers: number of New Accounts, number of Outstanding

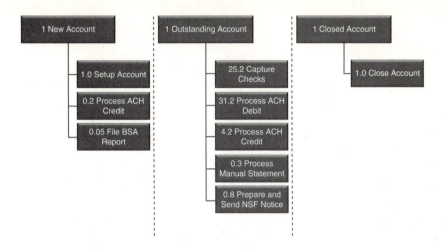

FIGURE 5.1 Simplified Master Driver Example

Accounts, and number of Closed Accounts, and several shared services drivers. In Figure 5.1, the activities are shown rather than the drivers. However, it is important to mention that this is a relationship between master drivers and other *drivers*, not activities per se.

Figure 5.1 shows the historical ratio between every outstanding account and the number of checks captured on a monthly basis is 25.2 to 1. Each outstanding account is expected to generate 25.2 checks per month. Similarly, the ratio between every outstanding account and the number of manual statements generated and sent is 0.3 to 1. For every ten outstanding accounts, three accounts will request a manual statement per month.

So, rather than requesting the Retail product group plan for every driver, Retail Product Managers need to plan for only the number of new accounts, outstanding accounts, and closed accounts by month. This is part of their normal expected planning process. These master drivers can then be multiplied by their historic ratios to determine operational-level drivers for operational planning purposes.

Figure 5.2 shows the final results of an annual plan in which the Retail unit planned the following: 23,000 new accounts, 845,000 outstanding accounts, and 5,200 closed accounts. Note that the two # of ACH Credits volumes shown under new accounts and outstanding accounts can be added together for operational planning purposes.

Master Drivers		Operational Drivers	Ratio
23,000 New Accounts			
	23,000	# of New Accounts	1.00
	4,600	# of ACH Credits	0.20
	1,150	# of BSA Reports	0.05
845,000 Outstanding Accounts			
	21,294,000	# of Checks Captured	25.20
	26,364,000	# of ACH Debits	31.20
	3,549,000	# of ACH Credits	4.20
	253,500	# of Manual Statements	0.30
	676,000	# of NSF Notices Sent	0.80
5,200 Closed Accounts			
	5,200	# of Closed Accounts	1.00

FIGURE 5.2　Master Driver Plan Results

Determining and Updating Master Driver Ratios

Master driver ratios for annual plans should be created based on the current year's actual ratios. These initial ratios are then modified to include specifically identified expected changes in the upcoming year. Common types of changes include the following.

Technology Shifts

An example of changing technology is the shift from paper check processing to image or ACH processing. In this case, the customer preference remains constant. They still write checks. However, checks may be converted to image or ACH by the customer, branch, or operations center.

In this example, using Figure 5.2, if the percentage of checks converted to image prior to reaching the operations center increases by 3%, the # of Checks Captured ratio would decrease from 25.20 to 24.44. The total number of expected checks would decline from 21,294,000 to 20,655,180 to reflect this 3% decline.

Additionally, the increase in the number of ACH debits is expected to increase 1% has a result of this shift. The # of ACH Debits ratio would increase from 31.20 to 31.51.

Customer Behavior Changes

The master driver ratios should be updated to reflect predictable customer shifts. Two examples include the shift from check and cash usage to debit and credit card usage and the "green movement" shift away from paper statements to online statements.

For this example, the shift from check usage results in another independent 2% drop in # of Checks Captured. Additionally, the shift results in an increase of debit card usage, increasing the # of ACH Debits ratio another 1%.

From a planning standpoint, let's assume the shift from paper statements to online statements results in a 5% reduction in manual paper statements. The master ratio for # of Manual Statements would decline from 0.30 to 0.29. With this small change, it is debatable whether the potential increased accuracy is worth the change to the master driver ratio. The answer is subjective. Does a decrease of approximately 13,000 manual statements per month change the staffing (or other resources) used by this activity? If so, change the master driver ratio.

Strategic or Process Shift

Strategic or process shifts reflect changes to your company's approach to the customer. An example of this type of shift is a change from mailing individual NSF notifications from one mailing per NSF to one NSF mailing per day (containing multiple NSFs by customer account). For our example, assume that this process change results in a decrease of 10% of the NSF notices sent. The master ratio for # of NSF Notices Sent would decrease from 0.80 to 0.72.

Regulatory Changes

Regulatory changes also impact the master driver ratios and can be clearly identified. For example, if the government requires stricter rules for counter-terrorism, the number of BSA reports would increase 20%. The master ratio for "number of BSA Reports" would increase from 0.05 to 0.06. Depending on the resources required, this increase of roughly 300 BSA reports per month may or may not be relevant to Operations.

Master Drivers	Operational Drivers		Ratio
23,000 New Accounts			
	23,000	# of New Accounts	1.00
	4,600	# of ACH Credits	0.20
	1,438	# of BSA Reports	**0.06**
845,000 Outstanding Accounts			
	20,229,300	# of Checks Captured	**23.94**
	26,891,280	# of ACH Debits	**31.82**
	3,549,000	# of ACH Credits	4.20
	240,825	# of Manual Statements	**0.29**
	608,400	# of NSF Notices Sent	**0.72**
5,200 Closed Accounts			
	5,200	# of Closed Accounts	1.00

FIGURE 5.3   Updated Master Driver Plan Results

Figure 5.3 summarizes all of the changes to the master driver ratios for all of the examples. Note that the total cumulative decrease of 5% is reflected in the # of Checks Captured ratio and the cumulative increase of 2% is reflected in the # of ACH Debits ratio.

Drivers for Commercial or Institutional Accounts

Master drivers work well in within Retail/Individual LOBs because of the homogeneous make-up of the customers. However, master drivers are not nearly as effective in Commercial/Institutional linLOBs due to the wide variety of large volume customers.

Generally, even prior to the implementation of ABC/M, product managers in Commercial/Institutional LOBs are required to plan at a driver level. The profitability and revenue plans for individual Commercial customers should be established based on the volume of lower level drivers. For example, within banking, volume projections such as the number of checks (broken out by local and nonlocal items), ACH debits, ACH credits, wires, statements, and cash orders/deposits (broken down by strapped currency, loose currency, etc.) are all incorporated into the sales proposals. Also, this line-item billing is delivered to the corporate customers on their monthly analysis statement.

Therefore, there are two primary sources of information for ABB planning purposes: sales proposals and current analysis statements, both of which are used by the product managers to plan and—depending on the size of the deal— should be in the Operations forecast.

Sales Proposals

As mentioned above, sales proposals should provide the detail for most operational drivers. Once again, depending on the size of the deal, Operations should not only be aware of the sales proposal, but should have assisted in the development of the proposal.

Two types of sales proposals are important to separate for planning purposes. First, examine the successful sales proposals that have closed within the past year. Are the volumes coming in as expected? What are the full-year implications of the actual volumes? Second, examine the sales proposal pipeline. Using some form of predictive modeling, determine the impact of these additional volumes, and, of course the Product and Sales management should estimate the impact of yet-to-be-identified sales. All of these operational drivers should tie to the Product and Sales managers' annual plans.

Analysis Statements

The monthly billing statements or "analysis statements" provide a great insight into two necessary sources of planning information: trending and potential attrition-related volumes. Analysis statements can indicate trends in individual customer behavior. Relationship managers should provide insight as to whether the trends will continue on a customer-by-customer basis as part of their normal planning process.

Also, similar to the sales pipeline modeling, known contract renewals with predicted attrition can be modeled and incorporated into the ABB planning. Once again, however, the sales and product plans drive the operational plan and should all reflect the same goals and assumptions.

INTEGRATING THE IT MODEL

Remember the old saying "One man's trash is another man's treasure"? Well, in activity-based costing, sometimes one model's cost object (output) is another model's resource (input). No place is this truer than the integration of the technology costs into the rest of the organization. Technology organizations within financial services generally view their services and products as output. Phone lines and support, personal computer hardware and support, projects and applications are all products and services delivered by IT. However, these products and services are viewed as resources (input) driven by other activities.

In this section, we will take a deeper dive into IT model integration. We will also walk through the pros and cons of three methods of application integration.

Phones, Personal Computers, and Projects

First, let's discuss a couple of the easier common IT cost objects: phones and personal computers (PCs). Both are considered resources for other activities and charged directly to cost centers throughout the organization. These cost center costs are then usually assigned to activities based on the use of personnel resources. This assignment is directionally correct. If 50% of an employee's time is assigned to Underwrite the Policy, then 50% of the resources used by this employee, such as the phone or PC, should go to Underwrite the Policy. Internal phone billing departments have a pretty straightforward task: Assign all phone usage costs by employee and cost center. Phone support costs, including PDA support costs, are generally assigned based on the number of devices by cost center. This is not perfectly accurate, but given the overall low costs for phone support, this is generally an appropriate simplifying assumption.

Similarly, PC costs are generally pooled and assigned based on the number of PCs by cost center. This includes the fully-bundled hardware, software, and licenses. During an ABC implementation, a senior leader challenged the PC costs assigned to his center. He pointed to his computer and said, "My PC does not cost exactly what is assigned to me." He was right. However, after a two-minute explanation of the value wasted in assigning over 30,000 unique costs for each PC, he realized the ABC team made a better decision by using a simplified rate structure (we used a basic and a premium rate, depending on the configuration of services). In this case, the climb was not worth the view.

Maintenance and Enhancement Projects

There are three varieties of Information Services (IS) projects: maintenance, enhancement, and new development. Maintenance and enhancement project costs for existing products and customers can be assigned through the ABC model in a fairly straightforward manner. In most financial services organizations, IS projects have their own general ledger account which makes the identification of these costs simple. Additionally, IS projects are generally a specific resource pool (in Chapter 3, IS projects was shown as a separate resource pool in Figure 3.1). In some cases, separate cost centers are used for IT charges. Use these situations to your advantage during the ABC implementation. The more isolated the IS projects are, the easier it is to use resource drivers to accurately drive these costs to the appropriate activities. Remember to use the IT billing system; it was designed to drive IT project costs to the correct LOB cost center(s) before using ABC to drive the costs to activities.

An alternative approach to assigning projects to activities, using unique resource drivers, is to assign project costs directly to the products supported by the project. While this provides accurate product costing, it requires a second step to assign these costs to customers (a "sideways" assignment or allocation within the cost object module). Given this complication, assigning projects to activities is a better alternative.

Development Projects

In the case of truly new development, no product or customer exists while the project is being undertaken. While the projects are still driven to the funding units, these units cannot assign cost through activities to cost objects. This is true even in the case of capitalized projects. There is still significant expense associated with capitalized project prior to release: Roughly 45% of the total project expenses will be recognized prior to implementation.

For all development projects, the project expenses should be assigned from the funding organization to the Non-Product, Non-Customer intersection of dimensions of their LOBs. These costs can then be sent to products and LOB customers as a "tax" (similar to overhead) or sent to a particular product group as a tax. For example, if the new product is a deposit product, it is more appropriate to tax only the products within the deposit product group.

Application Integration

Assigning application costs to products and customers can be one of the trickiest undertakings of an ABC/M project. The success of assigning applications depends on the objectives you are trying to accomplish. There are three main methods for assigning application costs: Each has potential pros and cons, depending on your objectives and your system constraints.

Application Integration Method #1: Applications as Resources

The first method is shown in Figure 5.4 and shows the applications treated just like the other IT cost objects. The IT cost objects become resources of the overall ABC model through direct IT chargeback to the cost centers.

The advantages of the Applications as Resources method include:

- From an ABC purist standpoint, it represents the fact that applications are just another resource consumed by the activities.
- It is consistent with the IT chargeback framework established for phones, PCs, and projects.

The disadvantages of the Applications as Resources method include:

- Depending on the user's and system's ability to trace back to the source of the cost, the application names may be "lost" in the assignment. This may or may not be important to understand during your implementation. During one major implementation,

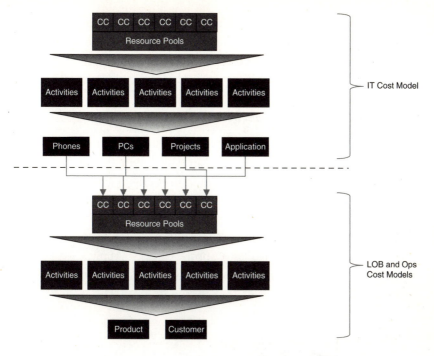

FIGURE 5.4 Application Assignment—Applications as Resources

we found it particularly helpful to be able to identify the application names associated with various products and activities. It was not only educational for the users, but enabled a dialog between LOBs, and IT then shut down infrequently used or obsolete applications. In order to maintain the application names throughout reporting, we were unable to use the Application as Resources method.

■ Like any large fixed cost with low-volume drivers, internally developed and maintained applications have a large fixed cost component (amortization) that can result in large variances if the activity drivers are low volume and highly variable. For example, Application X costs $200,000 per month to operate with a highly variable annual volume of 24,000 units. The expected rate would be $100/unit per month ($2,400,000/24,000 units). However, if the volume is highly variable and produces only 6,000 units in the first six months, there is an accumulated $600,000 variance between charges and actual costs ($1,200,000 – (6,000 units at $100/unit)). Depending upon the remaining forecast, this variance may need to be sent out to meet the full assignment needs of the organization.

Application Integration Method #2: Sister Activities

The Sister Activities method addresses some of the weaknesses of the Applications as Resources method and is shown in Figure 5.5. In essence, the Sister activities method requires creating several new activities that mirror existing activities. The only difference is the activity number and the inclusion of the application name at the end of the activity name. For example, the Capture Checks activity may have a sister application activity called Capture Checks: Application X. The Sister activity uses the exact same activity drivers as the original Capture Checks activity.

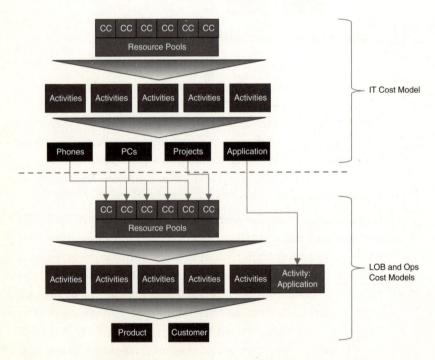

FIGURE 5.5 Application Assignment—Sister Activities

The advantages of Sister activities include:

- This method provides clear segmentation and identification of application costs assigned from activities to cost objects.
- It also maintains the same accuracy as the Applications as Resources method.

The disadvantages of Sister activities include:

- From an ABC purist standpoint, it "muddies the waters" between resources and activities.
- It is inconsistent with the IT chargeback framework established for phones, PCs, and projects.
- The issue with low-volume, highly-variable activity drivers described in Applications as Resources remains.
- If limiting rules are not established, this method results in an unmanageable increase in the number of activities. Imagine if every application within an organization was potentially assigned to each existing activity. The potential additional activities would be the total number of applications multiplied by the total number of activities. For example, if this method is used, use it only for the applications that represent the top 80% of the application spend and only allow each application a maximum of five Sister activities. This should keep your activities manageable, yet provide meaningful information to your users.

Applications Integration Method #3: Sister Activities with Fixed Drivers

In order to remove the residual issue associated with low-volume, high-variable activity drivers described in Applications as Resources, the Sister Activities method can be modified to drive costs out on a fixed driver basis. This flat month charge example is shown in Figure 5.6.

The advantages of Sister activities with fixed drivers include:

- This method provides clear segmentation and identification of application costs assigned from activities to cost objects.

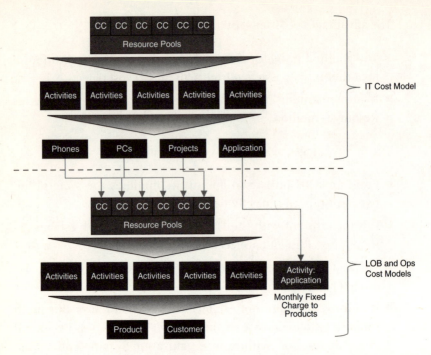

FIGURE 5.6 Application Assignment—Sister Activities with Fixed Drivers

■ It assigns a realistic and accurate cost to the products on a monthly basis with minimal residuals. For the most part, the residuals are the result of cost variances within the IT shared services unit.

■ Simplifies the activity drivers for all Sister activities by creating static annual "divide by twelve" activity drivers from the Sister activities to the products.

The disadvantages of Sister activities with fixed drivers include:

■ From an ABC purist standpoint, it "muddies the waters" between resources and activities.

■ It is inconsistent with the IT chargeback framework established for phones, PCs, and projects.

- Similar to the Sister activities method without fixed drivers, if limiting rules are not established, this method results in an unmanageable increase in the number of activities. Once again the challenge is to keep your activities manageable, yet provide meaningful information to your users.

- While this method simplifies and provides consistent product costing, it complicates customer costing. Customer costs now requires either (1) a two-step assignment from these sister activities, or (2) a split between assigned and unassigned customers.

  - In the two-step assignment, application costs are assigned to the product/unassigned customer cost object in the first step. The second step assigns (or allocates, depending on the method) costs from the unassigned customers to specific customers. It is very easy to lose traceability in this method.

  - If the assigned costs are split between known customer volumes and unassigned customer costs, an annual rate can be used for the known customer volumes. This provides consistent costs to the customers and forces the balance (either positive or negative) to the unassigned customer costs. This forces a balance between the customer and product dimensions. Traceability is maintained in this method.

As they say, "The devil is in the details." Sometimes when it comes down to the nitty-gritty in ABC, there is no perfect answer . . . just a trade-off between advantages and disadvantages.

DRIVING VALUE WITHIN SHARED SERVICES: IS EXAMPLES

Sometimes, ABC/M is implemented within an organization such as Information Services to help identify and quantify process improvements. In these situations, the ABC solution is used as a miniature data warehouse and financial calculator. At times, the insights can be gleaned from information outside ABC, but the resulting financial improvements cannot be accurately quantified without ABC. As food for thought, here are five examples of ABC-related output that identified ABM improvement recommendations.

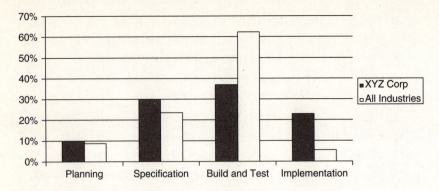

FIGURE 5.7 Application Development Comparison to External Benchmark

External Benchmarks: Application Development

In this example from an insurance company, the internal labor tracking data for application development was compared to external benchmark data from an international user's group. The results of external benchmarking are shown in Figure 5.7.

Notice the usually high effort in Implementation. After many interviews and examination of other data, the root cause was discovered. The Institutional LOB was continually attempting to meet unrealistic development timelines committed by the sales force. As you can imagine, some Institutional customers generated enough revenue to impact delivery timelines on a case-by-case basis. The Individual LOB, on the other hand, had no single customer powerful enough to influence the programming deadlines.

In order to meet the Institutional customer deadlines with the current staffing levels, the Institutional development programmers frequently rushed (and cut short) the testing phase of the system development life cycle. This led to two major issues: (1) increased costs associated with the Implementation as errors were continually being found while the applications were being installed, and (2) increased production errors, as we will see in the Normalized Production Errors example.

In this case, the ABC driver data identified the symptom in Figure 5.7. Subsequently, the ABC/M team determined the root cause and the ABC system quantified the expected value of the change.

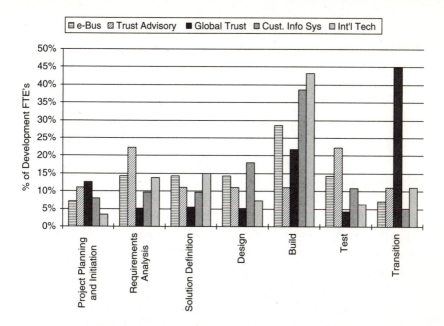

FIGURE 5.8   Internal Application Development Benchmark

Internal Benchmarks: Application Development

Improvement opportunities can also be identified by using internal benchmarks. In Figure 5.8, the application development areas of another company are compared to each other.

 Notice the extreme Transition effort within the Global Trust development team. The ABC/M interviewed and observed the process to determine the root cause. The Global Trust development team did not follow the corporate standard process for documenting requirements, solution definition, and design. This was verified in Figure 5.8 with minimal efforts in Requirements Analysis, Solution Definition, and Design. Design sessions were like informal agreements with the end-users.

 This loose process in the early phases led to problems during the Transition phase—specifically User Acceptance Testing (UAT). The users continually pushed back during UAT saying, "That is not what I wanted." Having no documentation to fall back on, the developers were at the mercy of the users until the users were satisfied their undocumented requirements were fulfilled.

Once again, the ABC driver data uncovered the problem. The ABC/M team determined the root cause and quantified the expected range of improvement.

Normalized Support Efforts

In some cases, the outlier is the leader. Figure 5.9 highlights a situation in which the Customer Information Systems support area implemented a "swat team" approach to resolving Tier 2+ errors: errors that require escalation beyond the centralized Help Desk (Tier 1 support).

Previous to the implementation of the "swat team" concept, Tier 2+ support consumed 4–5% of the available resources within each of the development areas. After the swat team implementation, the Customer Information System area redeployed resources to higher value-added activities. While the Net Income Before Taxes (NIBT) value was not specifically identified in this case, the bottom line impact could have been observed through a reduced reliance on contractors, for example.

It is important to note that this example, as well as the others, is based on normalized data. Specifically, in Figure 5.9, the relative percent of full-time equivalents (FTEs) is used to normalize for the common activities across development areas. The absolute number of FTEs is not used as the basis of comparison, since the larger development area is frequently the outlier due to its sheer size.

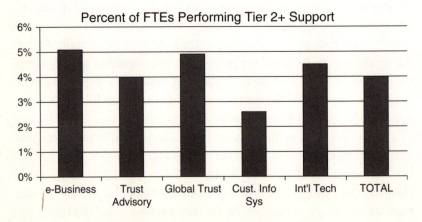

FIGURE 5.9 Normalized Internal Benchmark

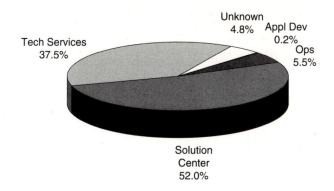

FIGURE 5.10 Help Desk Best Practice Comparison

Help Desk Best Practices

Some best (or leading) practices and metrics have fairly wide acceptance and, therefore, can be useful for comparison. Figure 5.10 compares Help Desk resolution to an external best practice goal recognized by the company of 66% first contact resolution.

The data clearly indicated that an additional 14% of the calls should be resolved by the less-costly support at the Solution Center. As a result of better Help Desk training, resulting in a deeper solution expertise and higher first contact resolution, Technical Services resources were redeployed to high valued-added activities.

Normalized Production Errors

For the last example, we return to the insurance company in highlighted in the External Benchmarks: Application Development section. As you recall, some Institutional customers pressured sales personnel to commit to unrealistic development deadlines. Not only was the development life cycle impacted, but the production quality suffered as shown in Figure 5.11.

Figure 5.11 clearly shows that while the Individual LOB had the most absolute errors (119 total errors for the time period), the Institutional LOB had more than five times as many errors for the time it ran on the mainframe. While it is difficult to prove with certainty that the

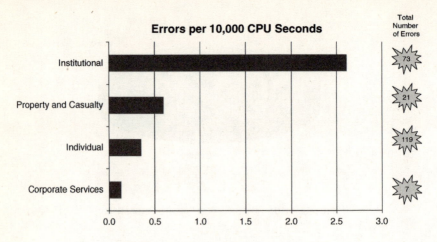

FIGURE 5.11 Normalized Production Errors

higher error rate was a result of rushed development and testing, the data indicates that the Institutional business was a negative outlier from a quality perspective. Also, many software development surveys have indicated that the cost of fixing production problems is eight times as expensive as discovering and fixing problems found in the Design phase. This "rule of thumb" was used to estimate the impact of reducing the Institutional error rate by roughly 80% or 58 errors.

This last example is unique in the fact that none of the driver data was created for ABC modeling. The driver data was imported and used in the model to drive mainframe and error-processing costs. While this information could have been discovered without implementing ABC, ABC surfaced an issue within the Institutional area which required more investigation into the drivers in an effort to prove or dispel the perceived quality problem. As a data aggregator, the ABC model contains a treasure trove of cost-and-effect relationships waiting to be discovered.

CHAPTER 6

Managing Organizational Change

It is not necessary to change. Survival is not mandatory.

—W. Edwards Deming

IMPORTANCE OF ORGANIZATIONAL CHANGE MANAGEMENT

While we all recognize the need to adapt and improve in order to grow and prosper, the resistance to change remains ingrained in all of us. This resistance is the primary reason why many accurate and well-designed ABC models are not converted into bottom-line results. Many ABC/M practitioners debate the merits of various ABC designs, but the best ABC model is still a waste of shareholder value without accompanying improvements.

Like many ABC/M implementers, I am a very numbers-oriented person. So, why do I emphasize a "soft skill" like organizational change management (OCM)? From a very practical standpoint, I believe in OCM because it increases the likelihood of ABM success.

FIGURE 6.1   Elisabeth Kübler-Ross' Five Stages of Grief

Reactions to Change

Elisabeth Kübler-Ross, in her book *On Death and Dying* (New York: Touchstone, 1969), unwittingly laid some of the foundation for OCM by defining the five stages of grief shown in Figure 6.1. Most people are familiar with the concept of the five stages and the stages have become common knowledge: Denial, Anger, Bargaining, Depression, and Acceptance.

Like any social science observation, the five stages are not a physical law. They are a framework and as a framework . . .

- The stages are not mandatory for grief.
- The stages have no predetermined "normal" amount of time.
- The stages are not necessarily linear. It is quite common to regress from Bargaining, for example, to Anger before moving to Depression.

Reactions to Business Change

Kübler-Ross' five stages have been modified over the past forty years to attempt to explain the natural resistance to change within the business world. Figure 6.2 is an example of a modified framework that reflects stages associated with business change: changes to people (organization), process, and technology.

While the particular stages and order of the stages in Figure 6.2 is debatable, there are several incontrovertible insights demonstrated by all of these types of OCM frameworks:

- There is a full spectrum of emotions that may be observed during change.

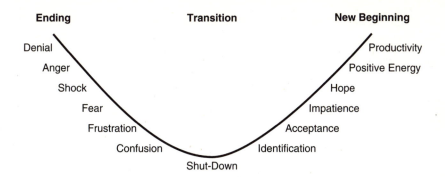

FIGURE 6.2 Example of Emotional Stages of Business Change

- Not all people go through the change process the same way. It is highly personal.

- There is generally a nadir for individuals during the change process. At this critical point, the employees either shut down or turn the corner. The lowest point is not a sustainable position.

- Just like the Kübler-Ross model, there is no standard time for the emotional stages.

- Also, just like the Kübler-Ross model, the model is not linear. People will frequently regress to earlier stages.

The first step in navigating the emotional stages of business change is to recognize they exist and are a process. The second step is assessing the resistance through examination of organizational alignment and readiness.

ORGANIZATIONAL READINESS AND OVERCOMING RESISTANCE

If you have ever been involved with a project requiring significant change, you have probably discussed the need to "create a burning platform" to enable change. If you have never heard the story behind the phrase "burning platform," here it is:

A man working on an oil platform in the North Sea was awakened suddenly one night by an explosion. Amidst the chaos, he made his way to the edge of the platform. As a plume of fire billowed behind him, he decided to jump from the burning platform even though he had been trained to never consider this as an option for the following reasons: It's a 150-foot drop from the platform to the water, and there are often debris and burning oil on the surface; and if the jump into the 40° F water doesn't kill you, you will die of exposure within 15 minutes. Luckily, the man survived the jump and was hauled aboard a rescue boat shortly thereafter. When asked why he jumped, he replied, "Better probable death than certain death."[1]

Most of the time, we do not have the motivation of a clearly fatal current state to drive changes. Therefore, many people first try to create a burning platform to motivate the change. However, before you start playing with matches, assess your current situation and determine if your burning platform needs to be just a small campfire or an inferno.

Evaluate the organizational readiness of the entire organization on several dimensions. Figure 6.3 shows some dimensions of change readiness. Where an organization falls on these spectrums indicate the

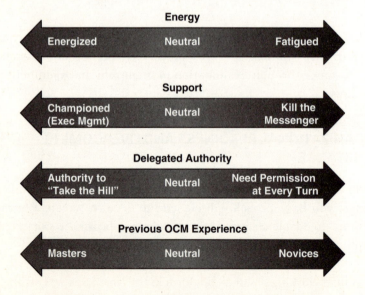

FIGURE 6.3 Qualitative Organization Readiness Assessment

type and amount of effort to put into the creation of the burning platform. One word of caution: Err on the side of a bigger fire; resistance is often underestimated.

While Figure 6.3 is not a quantitative tool, it does provide an interesting framework for qualitatively assessing organizational change readiness. After the more formal tools (shown later in this chapter) are used, refer again to this qualitative organization readiness assessment to get a sense of missed exposures.

Resistance to Change

Individuals resist change based on a combination of logical and emotional reasons. Some common reasons for resistance include:

- **Unresolved professional differences** This is the most logical reason for resisting change, but can also have an emotional side to it. If people *do not feel* their professional evaluations and opinions have been fully considered, they may resist the change. Often, people not only need to feel that they have been heard, but also need to understand that it is common to move organizations forward based on the concept of consensus, in which all viewpoints have had an opportunity to be aired and the final decision is expected to be supported by everyone. Consensus does not require unanimity or compromise.

- **Loyalty to the past** This is a type of melancholy. Disrespect of the past can be a very powerful emotional hurdle. I was working for IBM when the lifetime employment policy was ended. The CFO at that time addressed an audience in Poughkeepsie and stated that he had bad news and good news. The bad news was that "IBM is going broke." Now that's a burning platform! The good news was that "it will take a while and we have a chance to fix it." He had our attention.

- **Fear of the unknown** A little bit of rational fear can be motivational and drive people to succeed. A lot of fear—including irrational fear of the burning platform—can cause paralysis. Imagine if the oil worker in the burning platform situation had been paralyzed with fear. We certainly would not be extolling the virtues of building burning platforms. The paralysis threshold varies by individual, so be aware of this as you attempt to move people along the stages of business change.

- **Loss of power or influence** This resistance can also be a combination of logical (real loss) and emotional (perceived loss) influences. In any case, the individual *feels* like he or she is losing power and that is the important point. You may need to appeal to their sense of the "greater good" to overcome this resistance.

- **Peer pressure** Peer pressure is a bit of a strange resistance. By its very nature, it is secondary resistance, rooted in the support of someone else's resistance. Find the root cause of the resistance and overcome it. The peer pressure resistance should be overcome at the same time.

- **Personal change** We often forget about the baggage that people are unable to "leave at the door" when they arrive at work. If significant changes and stress are occurring outside of work—family issues, personal health issues, for example—people will tend to resist more changes at work. At times, people need some areas of their lives to be stable. There is no cure per se for this type of resistance. Recognizing and empathizing with the affected individuals helps both parties.

As shown above, there are many reasons for resisting change. However, there are basically two broad types of resisters: active and passive.

Active resisters provide straightforward resistance. They are generally vocal about their dissent and usually mount a frontal assault. This is the best type of resistance. The resistance is out in the open, the positions are stated, and the direct confrontation is hopefully not underhanded. Work together to try to overcome this resistance—as Stephen Covey pointed out in *The 7 Habits of Highly Effective People* (New York: Free Press, 2004), "Seek first to understand, then to be understood."

At times, active resisters can be a bit more devious—flanking your position by trying to get your peers to support their resistance or going over your head to attempt to block the change. Your first step is to indicate that you are aware of their efforts. This is done to get them to bring the issues out in the open, so they can be addressed.

Passive resisters are the hardest of the bunch. They are the type of people that say, "Yes, I understand and can have that information to you by Thursday." Of course, they leave the meeting muttering, "There's no way I'm sending that information by Thursday." Getting the reasons for resistance of these people out in the open is like driving snakes out of the tall grass. You spend a lot of time teasing them out, but you never know if you got them all. Once again, the key is bringing the issues out in the open, so they can be addressed. If an issue is not raised, it cannot be addressed.

Tools for Overcoming Resistance

Several tools exist for addressing and overcoming resistance. Given the variety of tools, templates, and approaches for addressing organizational resistance, I am reminded of the movie *Raiders of the Lost Ark*. In one scene, our hero, Indiana Jones, is confronted by one of the villain's huge henchmen. The henchman wields a large saber and puts on an impressive display of swordsmanship. It looks pretty bad for our hero. Indy looks down at his trusty bullwhip on his belt. Oh, wait . . . Indy notices his pistol on his other hip. He draws it and . . . bang! Another bad guy bites the dust. In the final shot of the scene, Indy sort of shrugs his shoulders as if to say, "Well, what did you expect me to do? The guy had a saber."[2]

The point is, our hero knew when to apply the correct tools. Every experienced product manager knows that tools should be applied selectively, based on the task at hand. So, as you review these change management tools, be cognizant of the fact that these tools may be overkill in some cases. These tools can be used to evaluate the overall ABC/M project or the individual ABM projects in the improvement portfolio. Use your judgment.

Stakeholder Assessment

The stakeholder assessment tool shown in Figure 6.4 is used to understand the overall importance and risk of stakeholders to the overall

Stakeholders (High-5, Medium-3, Low-1)	Power			Level of Concern				Other		Total Score
	Influences Others % Weight	Direct Control of Resources % Weight	Score	People % Weight	Process % Weight	Technology % Weight	Score	Product and/or Process Knowledge Score	Accessibility Score	
A			0.0				0.0			0.0
B			0.0				0.0			0.0
C			0.0				0.0			0.0
D			0.0				0.0			0.0
E			0.0				0.0			0.0

FIGURE 6.4 Stakeholder Assessment Tool

success of the project. Remember, stakeholders are all of the parties that have a vested interest in the outcome of your project. Stakeholders can include:

- Sponsors
- Customers
- End-users
- Internal functional groups
- Regulators
- Suppliers

As shown in Figure 6.4, use the tool to rank the stakeholders by the power they have over the project, the level of concern they have regarding the three solution components (people, process, and technology), their product and process knowledge, and their accessibility. The higher the total score, the more attention they require.

Force Field Analysis

One of my favorite resistance assessment tools is very simple. It represents a technique is called force field analysis. This tool is so simple it can be used formally (as shown in Figure 6.5) or informally by just thinking through the supporting and opposing forces. The action plans associated with force field analysis are pretty straightforward too: Accentuate the positive and eliminate the negative.

Figure 6.5 loosely represents the starting position of an actual improvement project at a bank. The concept was to remove the envelope deposits from the ATM two times per day, rather than the current single daily removal. We anticipated who would support the project from the start. The funding desk would support the project because it reduced the bank's daily funding needs. The float manager would support the project because it reduced the bank's float and this was part of his incentive. The loss prevention group would support the project because it reduced the amount of fraud losses. The line of business (LOB) CFO would support the effort because it was a solid business case.

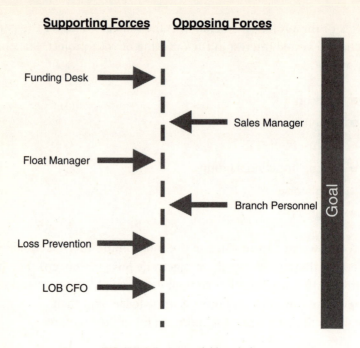

FIGURE 6.5 Force Field Analysis

And who would oppose the change? The sales manager would oppose the concept if he felt it interfered with the ability to sell. The branch personnel would also oppose the concept if they felt it was too time consuming and did not understand the benefit. Notice that the rationales behind both potentially opposing forces were known. The force field analysis indicated that we needed to provide facts to assist the supporting forces while investing the concerns of the opposing forces. In the end, the concerns of the opposing forces were allayed and the change was implemented.

Stakeholder Action Plan

Once the known and expected resistance has been documented, it is time to create mitigation plans to address and overcome this resistance. Figure 6.6 shows the template of an action plan created to overcome resistance. The purpose of the stakeholder action plan is to document resistance risks and mitigating actions, assign responsibility for

Stakeholder	Assessment Score (Power, Concern, Other)	Risks	Mitigating Actions	Responsible	Frequency, Start and End Dates
Executive Sponsor(s)					
Other Areas with the Process					
Product Management					
Loss Prevention					
Finance					
Customers					
Shareholders					
Internal Audit					
External Audit					
Suppliers					
Regulators					

FIGURE 6.6 Stakeholder Action Plan Template

executing the mitigating actions, and determine the frequency and timing of the mitigation plan. And just like any project plan, the stakeholder action plan needs to be monitored and adjusted throughout the project, as necessary.

YOUR ROLE AS CHANGE AGENT

Now that we have reviewed the reasons for OCM and some of the techniques and tools for overcoming the obstacles of change, what is your role in all of this? Depending on the size and scope of the ABC/M initiative, you may need to be the point person for ABC/M knowledge, project management, and OCM. That's a lot of hats! By owning the project deliver and the OCM, you are one of the most critical change agents within the ABC/M initiative. The executive sponsor also needs to be an active and visible change agent. But what is a change agent?

Attributes of a Change Agent

According to Answer.com, a change agent is "A person whose presence or thought processes cause a change from the traditional way of handling or thinking about a problem." This seems simple enough, but the definition misses a couple of key points. Being a change agent is not just about "presence" or "thought processes" it is about communicating and influencing (marketing and selling) to change the direction (i.e., make change) and make it stick.

To increase your ABC/M success you will need to develop change agent habits within yourself and your executive sponsor. If your own traits are not enough and you have the opportunity to augment your staff, recruit a change agent to help manage the organizational change.

The following are some common attributes of a change agent.

Passionate

This is not an artificial "rah, rah" passion that dies outside the room, but a passion rooted in the belief that the company will be in a much better place as a result of the change. You may require a few main change agents for the initial ABC implementation and other change agents for the individual ABM improvements. Passion for ABC as a whole may not translate into passion for an individual improvement and vice versa.

Energetic

It will take a lot of energy to implement ABC and the subsequent ABM improvements. The ABC project alone will probably take one to two years to implement. As we discussed earlier in this chapter, no one is fully capable of leaving his or her personal life outside of work. The change agent needs to be energetic over the course of the project, regardless of outside influences or distractions.

Future-Focused

The change agent is mentally living in the future and just visiting the present. He or she needs to reconcile current state (as is) to future state (to be) only in order to determine new and existing gaps and understand the ramifications to the future.

Optimistic

Change agents will encounter obstacles with people (such as those mentioned in the Resistance to Change section earlier in this chapter), process, and technology. These obstacles are encountered on day one and don't stop until the post-implementation review.

By having passion, energy, and optimism, the change agent is similar to the frog in the fable "The Frog and the Milk Bucket." As the fable goes, a frog was hopping around a farmyard, when it decided to investigate the barn. Being a bit too curious, he ended up falling into a pail half filled with fresh milk. As he swam about attempting to reach the top of the pail, he found that the sides of the pail were too high and steep to reach. He tried to stretch his back legs to push off the bottom of the pail but found it too deep. But the frog was determined not to give up, so he continued to struggle. He kicked and squirmed and kicked and squirmed. After a while, it became harder and harder for the frog to swim. He was about to give up. His final stroke felt like he was pulling the world. But, all his churning about in the milk had turned the milk into a big hunk of butter. The butter was now solid enough for him to climb onto and get out of the pail!

Change agents must be optimistic to believe that although the journey may become difficult, it will result in success.

Credible/Respected

For change agents to be effective, they must have followers. For the change agents to have followers, they must have organizational credibility and respect. Successful past implementations within the organization generally brings a lot of respect and credibility. Additionally, a track record of proven success outside the organization (such as previous implementations often cited by consultants) also establishes credibility and respect.

Empathetic

A great change agent reads people well and understands their desires and fears. These motivational buttons can be used to influence the direction and pace of change. Empathy is an honest understanding of another person, not just a manipulative tool. Honest empathy should be used to make win-win situations.

Excellent Communicator and Connector

Change agents need to inspire others through a communicated vision. The vision needs to grab stakeholders' hearts and convert them to believers, not just executors. Change agents need to connect emotionally with people. Great communicators have that ability.

Great Salesperson

The change agent needs to understand the difference between selling (obtaining buy-in) for the future state and overselling the future. Overselling is just not overstating the potential future, but continuing to sell well after the buy-in is established. Continuing to sell to converts can become stale and annoying. A good change agent knows the difference.

Your Deliverables

Now that we have discussed some of the attributes of change agents, let's discuss some of the deliverables you will be expected to create. This section is not a discussion about how to motivate and inspire others. Thousands of books have been written about these topics and are outside the scope of this book. Instead, this section provides examples of some specific change-related deliverables you will need to produce and manage.

Gap Analysis

Gap analysis is an extremely valuable assessment of the gap between the current state (as is) and the future state (to be). Structuring the gaps in terms of people, process, and technology is recommended, as these three dimensions represent the full picture of the solution.

From a practical standpoint, the gap analysis provides guidance for the project plan. For each gap, the project plan should contain steps to eliminate the gaps.

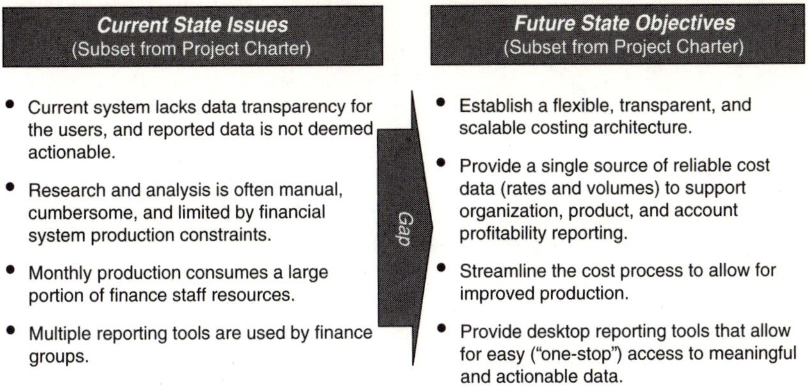

Current State Issues (Subset from Project Charter)	**Future State Objectives** (Subset from Project Charter)
• Current system lacks data transparency for the users, and reported data is not deemed actionable.	• Establish a flexible, transparent, and scalable costing architecture.
• Research and analysis is often manual, cumbersome, and limited by financial system production constraints.	• Provide a single source of reliable cost data (rates and volumes) to support organization, product, and account profitability reporting.
• Monthly production consumes a large portion of finance staff resources.	• Streamline the cost process to allow for improved production.
• Multiple reporting tools are used by finance groups.	• Provide desktop reporting tools that allow for easy ("one-stop") access to meaningful and actionable data.

Gap

FIGURE 6.7 High-Level Gap Analysis

From a change agent standpoint, the gap analysis bridges the current state to the future state. It begins to clarify the future state vision and provides some insight into the effort required to achieve the future state.

Figure 6.7 is a high-level gap analysis for communication purposes. While nearly 25 significant gaps were identified in the project charter, the four most visionary gaps were frequently communicated to inspire the organization and make the vision easy to remember.

Organizational Readiness Assessment

The organizational readiness assessment discussed earlier in this chapter is also one of your key tools as a change agent. It can be as simple as the qualitative organization readiness assessment in Figure 6.3 or as complex as a 30-page evaluation, depending on the size and complexity of the ABC/M initiative.

The organizational readiness assessment is a great planning tool. Like the gap analysis, it identifies weaknesses in the current organizational readiness early in the ABC/M project. Unlike the gap analysis, the organizational readiness assessment also provides strengths. These strengths can be levered to drive successful implementations.

Change Plan

Planning the change is not just creating the project plan. Planning the change involves your planned effort to move through the

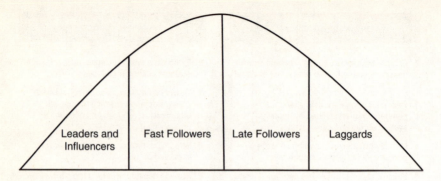

Leaders and Influencers   Fast Followers   Late Followers   Laggards

FIGURE 6.8   Change Adoption Curve

organizational change and bring the organization with you. Given the length of the ABC implementation, which milestones will be widely communicated and celebrated? Given the ongoing nature of the ABM project portfolio, how frequently should the milestones be realized in the beginning versus steady-state?

As part of the change plan, is it important to focus on different groups of people at different times in the ABC/M implementation. The change adoption curve shown in Figure 6.8 represents the different adoption rates for innovative products. This curve is a good proxy for the adoption of change within the organization. Too many change efforts focus on Late Followers and Laggards. However, successful change requires the initial focus to be on the Leaders and Influencers. Determine which people and areas are early in this upper quartile. Use them and their input for iterative design and testing prior to release into the general population. This group is used to seeing things on the leading edge and will provide valuable insight. Additionally, the upper quartile is frequently more accepting of initial solution glitches since they frequently adopt early innovations.

Communications Plan

One of the essential outputs from the stakeholder assessment is various types and frequencies of communication. These communication requirements should be consolidated into a communications plan. A sample abbreviated communications plan is shown in Figure 6.9. To be effective, the plan should contain the following:

Audience (Stakeholder)	Purpose (Need)	Frequency	Mode/Type	Start Date	Finish Date	Responsibility
Executive Sponsor(s)	Project status required to be informed	Weekly	E-mail summary	7/15/09	Project completion	Project Manager
Product Management	Project updates	Monthly	Word doc at meeting	7/31	Project completion	Project Manager
Customers	Send notices required by regulators	Once	Letter via US Mail	11/15	11/15	Corporate Communications

FIGURE 6.9   Sample Communications Plan

- Audience (Stakeholder)
- Purpose, need, or objective of the communication
- Frequency of the communication (hourly, daily, weekly, monthly, one-time, ad hoc)
- Mode or type of communication (face-to-face, phone call, meeting, e-mail, web posting, U.S. mail)
- Start date of the communication (when is the communication first delivered?)
- Finish date of the communication (when is the communication last delivered?)
- Responsibility(like all things, it is not a meaningful plan unless someone is responsible for doing the work)

On the surface, it may appear that the communications plan is not worth the effort. You could just as easily include these communications in the overall ABC/M plan. However, there are two major benefits of creating a separate communications plan.

First, the communications plan provides a snapshot of the communications (and only the communications) in one spot. Seeing all of the communications together will highlight inconsistencies, redundancies, and missed opportunities.

Second, when viewed and managed as a complementary effort, the communications plan can be managed by a single communications specialist, who can improve the overall quality and effectiveness of the ABC/M messaging.

NOTES

1. www.qualitydigest.com/march97/html/66side2.html
2. From what I remember, the actual reason for the abbreviated fight scene was that Harrison Ford was not feeling well during the shooting of the scene. So, in order to end the day early, the director agreed to change the script to allow Indiana Jones to shoot the bad guy, rather than using his trusty bullwhip.

CHAPTER **7**

Avoiding the Pitfalls: Lessons Learned

There are three kinds of men. The one that learns by reading. The few who learn by observation. The rest of them have to pee on the electric fence to see for themselves.

—Will Rogers

Over many years and through many implementations, you either learn a few lessons about implementing ABC/M or you lose your mind—there is not a lot of middle ground. Fifteen years ago, there were few documented lessons learned about ABC/M implementations. Thankfully, that has changed. If you happen to be one of the rare people who learn more from reading than from self-discovery, this chapter is for you! On the other hand, if you need to feel the power of the electric fence to understand it hurts, consider this chapter a bit of a warning before the "zapping" sensation.

ABC LESSONS LEARNED

You will encounter and make literally hundreds of design decisions during an ABC implementation; there are seven lessons learned that

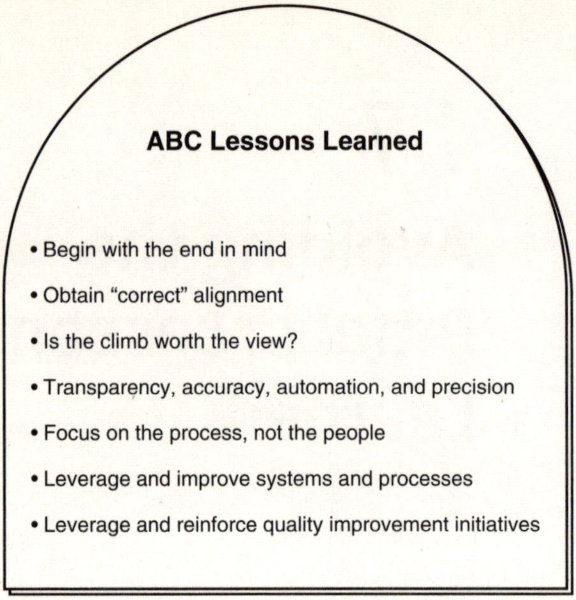

ABC Lessons Learned

- Begin with the end in mind

- Obtain "correct" alignment

- Is the climb worth the view?

- Transparency, accuracy, automation, and precision

- Focus on the process, not the people

- Leverage and improve systems and processes

- Leverage and reinforce quality improvement initiatives

FIGURE 7.1 ABC Lessons Learned

can guide your decision-making process. These lessons learned are shown in Figure 7.1.

Begin with the End in Mind

In Chapter 3, several ABC implementation guiding principles were introduced. One theme underlying several of the guiding principles is "Begin with the end in mind." Who will be accountable for changing processes, products, and customer behaviors based on the ABC information? How will they be held accountable? What types of information will they need? How will the data be delivered? Is there an opportunity to make this an iterative development process to generate quick wins?

As your company's visionary ABC leader, you need to know the answers to these questions in order to describe the future state and inspire others to reach this "house on the hill." Clearly, project management is essential for day-to-day and month-to-month progress, but you need to know where you are headed before you begin the journey.

Obtain "Correct" Alignment

If ABC/M is viewed as only an accounting project, the bottom line impact will be very limited. Unfortunately, this narrow view of ABC/M as an accounting effort is not uncommon. During one implementation, Information Technology (IT) management tried to convince executive management that ABC/M was an IT project. However, ABC/M is a *business* project which requires IT enablement. Overall, project management and sponsorship need to reside in the area accountable for improving the bottom line using ABC data.

In Chapter 2, this book discussed the scope of ABC/M. The best and most appropriate sponsorship sits at the highest level of the scope. For example, if the ABC/M scope is enterprise-wide, the CEO needs to be the project sponsor. This sponsorship needs to include all of the textbook duties of a sponsor including, but not limited to: active and visible support, assignment of resources, and removal of barriers. The sponsor should have the authority to include the success of the ABC/M implementation in the performance plans of the key constituents of the ABC/M effort. Include ABC/M delivery and bottom line results in performance plans to ensure goal alignment.

Is the Climb Worth the View?

So, you have painted the house on the hill and have appropriate sponsorship. What about the myriad of detailed data, analysis, and reporting people will try to add along the way? You will need a method of quantitatively and qualitatively estimating the costs and benefits of these alternatives. Additionally, you will need a steering committee (or ABM Board) to help resolve these choices.

Here are a few typical requests:

■ **"We would like to see 'Perform General Administrative Activities' as a separate activity"** This may be a valid request to help provide an accurate benchmark. However, who will be accountable for managing/improving this activity? What will this additional activity, which must be re-assigned to determine a fully-loaded cost, do to the performance and usability of the system?

■ **"We would like to see tiered rates for application development"** This request is a bit dubious if it comes from the line of business (LOB). Will the LOB determine application development staffing? This request generally occurs when the LOB is frustrated with the costs and value of its application development area. I successfully convinced three large financial services firms that tiered rates are counterproductive. It is better to augment and improve the ABC data with function point[1] data (for example) to baseline and benchmark application development efficiency and productivity.

As your ABC/M effort evolves, you may need to modify your approach: "If the map differs from the terrain, follow the terrain." So, for example, if you enabled the LOBs to see the fixed and variable expense components for the shared services organizations and the LOBs do not use the data to improve the business, you have two choices: (1) increase your efforts to make the LOBs accountable for improving shared services costs through the use of fixed and variable information, or (2) shut down this ability—which will save production and reporting resources. You need to optimize the balance between information production efforts and bottom line results from information usage.

Transparency, Accuracy, Automation, and Precision

Two common pitfalls in ABC implementations are a lack of transparency (sometimes it even becomes downright secrecy) and a premature drive to automation.

As shown in Chapter 2, the order of transparency, accuracy, automation, and precision is important. The pitfalls are straightforward. A lack of transparency leads to distrust in the data and a plethora of questions regarding the ABC calculations and drivers. This results in more investigative work by the ABC implementation team. Assuming you have created a high quality ABC model, transparency allows users to "kick the tires," validate the results, and point out opportunities for improvements.

Similarly, attempts to prematurely automate the system can be a waste of project resources. In the beginning, use "good" existing automated sources (including proxy drivers) in lieu of "better" manual sources that require significant automation effort. After the ABC data has been validated and it is clear the data will be used, prioritize the automation of drivers applying the "Is the climb worth the view?" method. It makes no sense to automate a data source that is not used or is marginally useful.

It is not uncommon for users to question the accuracy of the ABC model. Embrace the conversation as long as it is constructive. If there are ways to improve the model accuracy with little increased effort, make the changes. However, if users maintain the ABC model is not "right" but have no helpful improvement suggestions, be very cautious. You probably have an organizational change management (OCM) issue on your hands. There are product managers that are not comfortable making decisions with 90%+ accurate information and will challenge the "accuracy" of the ABC model. Generally, it is an attempt to undermine the credibility of the model with vague insinuations that if they could really do a better job if only the ABC model were 100% accurate. To combat this situation, communicate early and often that ABC or any other costing system will never be 100% accurate. It is not a realistic or desired outcome of any costing system. Do you need to know the exact cost of my candy bar versus yours to make an informed decision about process and cost improvements? People need to be comfortable making decisions with 90%+ accurate information. In particular, if product managers are not comfortable making decisions with 90%+ accurate information, they are probably in the wrong job.

Focus on the Process, Not the People

Quality and process experts including W. Edwards Deming and Joseph Juran noted that in most systems 80–85% of the outcomes are due to the process and only 15–20% are due to the worker. Deming demonstrated this concept for decades in his famous Red Bead Experiment.

In a typical Red Bead Experiment, Dr. Deming selected several "workers" from the audience. The workers were each asked to draw fifty beads from a bowl using a special paddle. The bowl contained 20% red beads representing defects and 80% white beads representing quality output. Dr. Deming diligently tracked all results on a flip chart. After the first round, the best workers, based on the high number of white beads, were given raises and some of the worst workers were fired. Usually, in the second round of bead selection, a few of the best workers in the first round did not perform as well. These workers got a performance notice and stern lecture from Deming. By this point, the absurdity of the reward system was apparent to the audience. While the reward system was very measurable and well-defined, it was still based on a random distribution of errors imbedded in the process. Without changing the process, the workers continued producing a normalized distribution of errors with a mean error rate of 20%. Workers were rewarded or punished based on the inherent process, not their controllable contribution to the outcome (which was zero in this case).

Even though most people recognize that logically the process is responsible for the results, in many cases people are rewarded or punished as if they were the majority contributors of the outcome. Sales personnel are commonly both beneficiaries and victims of this misguided thinking.

A clear example of overcompensation of sales personnel was seen during the go-go years of the home mortgage business from 2001 to 2007. Mortgage brokers throughout financial services routinely received large commissions for merely fulfilling order requests. How difficult was it to convince someone to take out a 4.5% fifteen-year fixed mortgage? Or an interest-only mortgage? The phone was ringing off the hook because of market conditions, including a pervading misperception of low risk—not because the mortgage brokers had become great salespeople overnight. However, the industry treated the mortgage brokers like rainmakers.

The quality field understands that most results are process-driven, including sales. The ABC team needs to follow this philosophy, as well, for two very important reasons. First, only by changing the process will you materially and permanently change the results. Second, focusing on the process takes a lot of the emotion associated with personal pride out of the equation. People want to perform meaningful and quality work. Any implication to the contrary is an attack on their value and sense of worth. How to focus on the process is addressed in the "Never Call the Baby Ugly" section later in this chapter.

Leverage and Improve Systems and Processes

The ABC system needs data. It is a classic GIGO (garbage in, garbage out) system. If the driver input is accurate and timely, the ABC output will be more accurate and timely. Therefore, leverage every opportunity to use and improve existing resource and activity driver sources.

IT Resource Utilization Systems

IT shared services have two common sources for resource and activity drivers: labor tracking systems and job scheduling systems. These two sources can drive the majority of IT expenses.

Labor tracking systems, such as Clarity or Planview, capture the application development time by a work breakdown structure (WBS) and project number. Typically, the WBS is based upon a common system development life cycle (SDLC). In layman's terms, all projects follow the same major steps. These steps are similar to the following seven generic application development steps, in life-cycle order:

1. Plan and Initiate Project
2. Gather Requirements
3. Define Solution
4. Design Solution
5. Build Solution
6. Test Solution
7. Implement Solution

The SDLC used at your company can be mapped to generic application development steps like these, or they can be maintained in the company's own SDLC. These seven generic steps comprise the activities in the ABC model.

There are two advantages to mapping to generic development steps. First, it enables better discussion between the LOBs and IT. LOBs can usually understand the seven steps listed above. The mapping translates the fancy tech-speak of the SDLC to common business terms. Second, if you plan to compare the labor tracking results to external benchmarks, the generic steps lend themselves to comparison better than company-specific steps.

ABC can be used to reinforce the use of the labor tracking system, too. Total available hours can be compared to tracked hours. Remember, if the labor hours are billed to LOBs by project, the head of application development has a vested interest in accounting for all billable hours.

Effective use of the labor tracking system in application development will provide ABC with the resource drivers (resource hours by activity), activity drivers (activity hours by project), and unbilled hours (unused capacity) which are managed by the application development managers. Additionally, labor tracking systems are frequently used by IT operations. If this is the case, work with IT operations to develop tracking by activity. Once again, the labor tracking system should provide both resource and activity drivers.

Staffing Models

Branch and operations (non-IT) staffing models can be beneficial in ABC implementations. The best staffing models are based on time studies. As mentioned several times throughout this book, the time study data can be used to create volume-based resource and activity assignments with calculated unused capacity.

If the time study data is stale or of little value to the ABC model, revise the time study to meet the needs of both the ABC model and the staffing model requirements.

Capital Expenditures Approval Process

The capital expenditures (Cap Ex) process is a commonly overlooked process in ABC implementations. However, the process can provide extremely valuable forecasting information to the ABC model. Similarly, the ABC model can provide extremely valuable information to estimate business cases within the Cap Ex process.

As an example, while seeking approval to implement a project to reduce fraud and improve fee income, the project team estimated an increase in nonsufficient funds (NSF) notices. As you would expect, the Number of NSF Notices was the activity driver for Prepare and Send NSF Notices within Operations. An increase in the number of NSF notices required additional resources—namely personnel, paper, envelopes, and postage. The draft business case had overlooked these additional resource expenses. The revised business case included the predicted results from ABC to create a more comprehensive and accurate business case for the project.

Since most projects are undertaken to improve business performance, and most business performance metrics are ABC resource and/or activity drivers, modify your company's capital expenditure requests to include the expected quantifiable impact on ABC drivers. These changes to drivers are quantified business objectives and need to become part of the capital expenditure and post implementation review process.

Customer Relationship Management Systems

Potentially information-rich sources of driver data are Customer Relationship Management (CRM) systems. CRM systems can provide a history of the sales efforts (activities) by customer and product. In particular, the pipeline activities can be incorporated into the model to determine the cost of unsuccessful sales activities and, more importantly, the unit cost of both successful and unsuccessful sales activities. Process improvements can be made to weed out unsuccessful sales earlier in the sales process, which effectively increases the pipeline capacity.

CRM still has many years to go before achieving its potential within financial services. Reinforcing the importance of the CRM data by using the data in the ABC model is a win-win. It improves the accuracy the CRM data which benefits the sales process and product/customer cost accuracy within the ABC system.

Leverage and Reinforce Quality Improvement Initiatives

Just as existing systems and processes can be utilized and reinforced by the ABC system, quality improvement initiatives should have a mutually beneficial relationship with ABC. For example, as discussed in Chapter 3, activities can be tagged with attributes to enable Six Sigma analyses. The ABC team and the Six Sigma team have common goals including:

- Reducing process variability, thereby improving process repeatability and predictability
- Eliminating waste through process improvement
- Reducing costs through process improvement

Design the ABC system to enable both Six Sigma and ABM improvements.

In Chapter 4, we briefly discussed how the balanced scorecard can be used to prioritize the ABM project portfolio. However, ABC can be beneficial to the balanced scorecard as well. Specifically, activity costs and drivers can be used as metrics within the balanced scorecard. For example, through the use of ABC, error-related activity costs can be viewed on a monthly basis and included as a tracking metric for the Internal Business Process perspective. Additionally, customer and product profitability may be key metrics in the Financial perspective.

One word of caution: Leverage and reinforce *solid* quality improvement initiatives. That is easier said than done. You need to recognize the difference between (1) strong quality improvement initiatives that could assist the ABC effort, (2) moderate quality improvement efforts that have a legitimate chance of success with the assistance of ABC, and (3) quality improvement efforts with no real chance of success.

If you cannot avoid teaming with doomed improvement efforts, the ABC initiative may suffer reputational damage through "guilt by association."

ABM LESSONS LEARNED

Similar to the ABC lessons learned, there are also several ABM lessons learned to guide your decision-making process. As shown in Figure 7.2, these seven lessons learned emphasize organizational alignment, project management, and team leadership.

Never Call the Baby Ugly

> It is not the critic who counts: not the man who points out how the strong man stumbles or where the doer of deeds could have done better. The credit belongs to the man who is actually in the arena, whose face is marred by dust and sweat

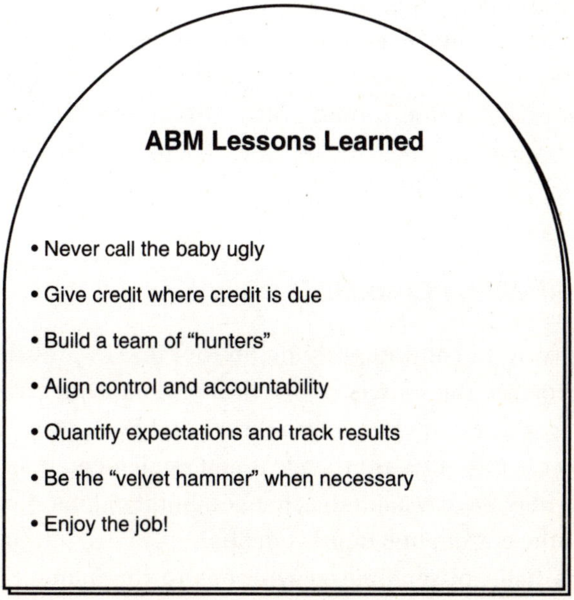

ABM Lessons Learned

- Never call the baby ugly
- Give credit where credit is due
- Build a team of "hunters"
- Align control and accountability
- Quantify expectations and track results
- Be the "velvet hammer" when necessary
- Enjoy the job!

FIGURE 7.2 ABM Lessons Learned

and blood, who strives valiantly, who errs and comes up short again and again, because there is no effort without error or shortcoming, but who knows the great enthusiasms, the great devotions, who spends himself for a worthy cause; who, at the best, knows, in the end, the triumph of high achievement, and who, at the worst, if he fails, at least he fails while daring greatly, so that his place shall never be with those cold and timid souls who knew neither victory nor defeat.

Teddy Roosevelt,
"Citizenship in a Republic,"
Speech at the Sorbonne, Paris, April 23, 1910

One of the best pieces of advice I received in my consulting years was, "Never call the baby ugly." No one is interested in hearing how bad the current situation, process, product, or customer is. As a matter of fact, some of the people in the room may have had an active role in creating this ugly baby and are very proud of it. Like Roosevelt's quote above, it is very difficult to create processes, products, and customers and much too easy to criticize the results.

On the other hand, everyone should be interested in hearing how to make the baby better looking. How much better can it be made for how much effort (value proposition)? Give them the next steps in milestone format to make this possible. Focus on ideas and plans to make the baby better looking.

Give Credit Where Credit Is Due

The easiest way to continue driving bottom line improvements is to publicly recognize the sources of the ideas and implementation teams. In today's world of corporate intranet sites and groupware, this is easier than ever before. Reward the ideas and implementations appropriately. ABM may have *enabled* the changes, but it did not recognize nor implement the bottom line improvements.

Make a habit of sending recognitions to the managers of those folks that used ABM to identify and implement bottom line improvements. It is human nature to repeat behaviors that receive praise.

Conversely, the best way to shut off bottom line improvements is to take undeserved credit. Simply put: Don't do it.

Build a Team of "Hunters"

"Hunters" are people that spend the majority of their waking hours either improving the bottom line or thinking about how to improve the bottom line. They have a mentality that they need to earn their paycheck on a daily basis. Hunters are people that think of improvement ideas as they go to bed and jot them down. Hunters think up solutions in the shower and on the drive into work.

The ABM team should be challenged to identify and implement ten times their costs. Use the entire cost center's costs to set the bar for the team. Encourage teamwork by using the team goal for everyone.

Beware of staffing an ABM office with "in basket/out basket" people. These people wait for items to enter their "in" basket and work the items to the "out" basket. When five o'clock rolls around, they are nowhere to be found.

Ideally, the hunters and in/out basket people are identified in the interview process. Any example of a question that helps identify hunters is "Tell me about a time when you really felt successful?" Drill down on the answers to determine their passion for idea generation and, more importantly, execution.

Align Control and Accountability

After structuring ABM to incentivize overall behavior, the most common remaining obstacles are misalignments of control and accountability. Control/accountability misalignments surface over and over again. Here are a few examples:

■ An idea was surfaced to increase LOB revenue by nearly $3 million (LOB accountability), but the shared services organization would have to increase staffing to handle a mere ten hours more work per week (shared services control). Naturally, shared services had incentive to keep staffing low and no incentive to increase LOB revenue.

■ At a bank, the branches controlled the cash orders and, therefore, the cash inventory at the branches (control). However, a centralized cash logistics team was accountable for total cash levels at the bank (accountability). Since there was no income statement cost to the branches of holding excess cash, they held millions more at the branches than was necessary to meet customer needs.

■ At a company without a politically strong Product Management team, Sales set pricing by utilizing exception pricing (control) without Product Management approval. However, the product managers were accountable for product profitability (accountability). This resulted in exception rates much higher than industry average.

■ Within banking, there is a particularly strange deep-rooted phenomenon: People are compensated higher for making loans than for gathering cheap deposits. This is strange because deposit products are generally more profitable and involve lower risk. The primary risk of deposits is fraud which, in the grand scheme of things, is pretty well controlled and, by definition, requires illegal behavior on the part of the customer. However, loans have default risk which is not nearly as controllable and requires no illegal behavior on the part of the customer. Most default loans occur to people that would actually like to make the payment, but cannot.

By motivating people to sell more loan products than deposit products, some undesirable behavior takes place: People will sell deposit products as loss leaders just to make loans. Rather than sacrifice loan spread revenue and a lower compensation for them, some relationship managers will steeply discount the deposit (cash management) services. Since the relationship managers are often compensated on credit volume and spread, they win. Since cash managers are often compensated on revenue, they win, too. But, since the entire relationship is less than the required return on equity, the shareholder losses in two ways: (1) economic value is destroyed by the relationship, and (2) people are paid incentives to destroy this value which, of course, destroys even more value.

Here are three lessons learned on how to avoid this particular double loss for the shareholder:

1. Do not allow sales personnel to exception price without Product Management approval. This holds true for all products.
2. Allow only pricing exceptions based on the expected current and future value of the customer.
3. When exceptions are requested on the deposit products that destroy shareholder value, ask the relationship manager why the exception is not taken exclusively on the credit spread. Exceptions on either product group—credit or deposit—will be the same from customer and shareholder perspectives. Both types of exceptions take value from the shareholder and give it to the customer. However, only deposit exceptions have the potential to maintain incentives for both relationship and cash management sales personnel.

In some cases, the accountability is not misaligned per se, but is placed on less than ideal behaviors. Often, these behaviors conflict with performance desired by shareholders. A few examples include:

■ Product managers are often compensated (accountability) based on revenue growth. Revenue growth is not a primary benefit to the shareholder. Instead, long-term value creation is the desired shareholder outcome. Revenue growth is influenced by many factors outside the control of product managers including corporate strategy, incentive plans, and uncontrollable market influences. The shareholders would be better served if product managers were compensated based on product profitability. Usually, the product manager has more influence on product expenses (control) and this aligns product manager goals to shareholder goals.

■ If branch profitability is not based on servicing and owning branches with credit offsets between the branches, branch profitability will be distorted (as shown in Chapter 2). This distortion may lead to closing heavy servicing branches which, in turn, results in much higher than expected account losses throughout the branch network.

Fortunately, all of the above examples can be resolved by bringing the misalignments out in the open and finding a way to improve the bottom line without negatively impacting the group in control. The ABM Board meeting is appropriate for this type of discussion.

Quantify Expectations and Track Results

Did everyone understand the definition of "winning" before we started?

It is important for you and your team to set the right expectations early in the ABM implementation. These expectations define your success or failure. The most important expectations you need to quantify are those regarding timing and value (Net Income Before Taxes). The ABM Board needs to know when to expect results and how much value to expect. When estimating the timing and value of the initial ABM portfolio, be conservative. As is the case in much of life, it is much better to underpromise and overdeliver.

How do we know we are winning or losing if we are not keeping score?

Unlike preschool soccer games, score is being tracked every day in the business world whether you like it or not. The final scores are printed daily in the financial press and are represented by your company's share price.

You need to track the results of the ABM initiatives on a monthly and yearly basis and publish the results. Several quantification and tracking tools were discussed in Chapter 4 and are available on this book's companion website. Remember, your results need to be validated by an objective party. Enlist the Finance staff independently to verify and validate (audit) the ABM improvements.

Be the "Velvet Hammer" When Necessary

Speak softly and carry a big stick; you will go far.

—Teddy Roosevelt

Once again, Teddy Roosevelt was right. Implementing improvements (ABM or any other) can be difficult, so you need to carry a big stick. It is best if this stick is in the form of heavy sponsorship through the ABM Board or the highest appropriate sponsor. If it is widely known that you have the ear of the executives, you can speak softly and be very effective.

If differing opinions need to be escalated to the ABM Board, let the people representing the other perspective know that you are obligated to surface the differing opinions to the ABM Board. Invite the differing opinions to the ABM Board to present their case.

Sometimes you may have to practice diplomacy as defined by Will Rogers: "Diplomacy is the art of saying 'Nice doggie' until you can find a rock." By arranging your support prior to encountering any obstacles, you will be following some additional advice which is "When possible, gather your rocks (sticks or hammers) before you meet any dogs."

Enjoy the Job!

Change is difficult and you are asking people to change every day during an ABM implementation. Organizational and process change is what makes ABM implementation challenging and exciting. Frankly, most people cannot do it well. Take pride in the fact that you are driving shareholder value. Remember, deep down, people want to do the right thing and provide value. They may need a little structure, convincing, and prodding. That is your role!

NOTE

1. Function points are a method of measuring the software development and testing efforts. Combining effort information from function points and cost information from ABC results in a financial efficiency measurement. Cost per function point is an excellent example of a normalized baseline measurement in IT.

CHAPTER 8

Beyond ABC/M

Whatever you undertake, act with prudence, and consider the consequences.

—Anonymous

PORTABLE SKILLS

In any role, you develop job-specific skills and portable skills. Job-specific skills are "deep" skills that enable you to become an expert in a particular field or topic. Subject matter experts (SMEs) spend years honing job-specific knowledge and skills. Portable skills, on the other hand, are more suitable to most of today's careers. Portable skills are "wide" skills that will help guarantee lifetime *employability*, not lifetime employment with a single employer or single role within an employer.

Both job-specific and portable skills have advantages. If you ever need life-saving surgery, you would probably like the surgeon with the best job-specific skills: an expert in the field with more than ten thousand hours of experience. On the other hand, portable skills are more important in an industry like consulting. In this case, attitude and adaptability are more important than aptitude. As a successful consulting senior manager, I have repeatedly delivered strong project results by staffing project teams with a minimum of 30% strong in portable skills—smart, hard-working, results-focused, team players were much more valuable than experts who may be lacking these attributes. In the worst case, the remaining 70% of the team are trained and led by the strong 30%. Depending on the size of the project, between one and three SMEs are required to deliver great results.

Planning, implementing, and managing successful ABC/M projects and organizations develop strong job-specific and portable skills. Whether you choose to continue a career in costing (job-specific) or undertake other bottom line impactful changes is up to you. The remainder of this section describes many of the portable skills you may develop as part of the ABC/M initiative.

Product Profitability

Owning full product profitability is one of the keys to successful product management. Full product profitability entails control and accountability for improving customer, front office and back office processes, cost structures, and pricing. Valuable product profitability experience obtained during an ABC/M implementation is very portable. Product and service profitability is required at nearly every company and across industries.

Customer Segmentation and Profitability

Similar to product profitability, ABC/M can provide a lot of valuable insight into customer segmentation and profitability. As shown in Chapter 4, focusing on customer behavior can result in significant bottom line improvements. Since most companies provide value by selling a variety of products and services to many customers across many different markets, segmenting these customers and markets to maximize profitability is an extremely useful and portable skill.

Project Planning

"Plan your work. Work your plan. Your plan will work." This is the standard mantra for project planning and execution. Project planning is a valuable portable skill, even if you do not decide to pursue a career in project management. Since businesses only get better through change, and successful change requires project planning and execution, you will be either delivering projects or receiving project deliverables throughout your career. In either case, it is important to understand basic project management philosophies and skills required for project delivery, including project planning.

Organizational Change Management

One of the most difficult and rewarding challenges of implementing ABC/M is organizational change. Establishing and reinforcing bottom line results through the use of an ABM Board or steering committee are portable skills and practices. Want to improve your company's liquidity (accounts receivable and accounts payable)? Establish the same structure outlined in this book for the ABM Board. Make the default answer on improvement projects "yes" rather than "no." Place the burden of proof on those wishing to stop improvement projects rather than the other way around. It is an amazing, eye-opening, cultural change.

Project Prioritization and Portfolio Management

In computer design terminology, "thrashing" represents an undesired state in which a computer system is overwhelmed. It has a high number of tasks to complete and very little time to dedicate to each task. In essence, all of the time dedicated to a task is exhausted just setting up to perform the task. The most effective way to break a thrashing state is to execute a single task to completion and then move to the next task—a temporary move away from multitasking to single-treading in order to break the logjam caused by the thrashing state.

Similarly, in the business world, thrashing occurs when individuals are pulled in too many different directions at once and cannot dedicate enough time to any particular task to make overall progress. Successful ABC/M implementation requires using a method for project prioritization. This is a portable skill and can be used at work or in your personal life.

Project portfolio management is also a portable skill that is broader than project prioritization. Project portfolio management, as discussed in the book, includes project selection and tracking. It can be used whenever the resources required to complete a portfolio of projects is less than the current available (or desired) resources.

Process Improvement

Process improvement and quality movements have taken on many names over the past twenty years including: Quality Circles, Do It Right the First Time (DIRTFT), Business Process Re-engineering, Focused Improvement, Workout, Six Sigma, Lean Manufacturing, and Lean Six Sigma. There is merit in each of the concepts. Also, like any good idea, these concepts are at risk of being overused or misused—used to resolve nonprocess issues or used without appropriate management support, for example.

Process mapping, decomposition, and improvement are all portable skills. When process improvement concepts are supported with the tools and techniques identified and discussed in this book, you will get bottom line improvements.

Business Case Development

Finance is the language of business. To have long-term success in business, learn to speak the language. Unless you become proficient at making business cases, you will have difficulty convincing Upper Management and Finance to invest time and funding in your uncovered opportunities. What are the Net Present Value (NPV), the Internal Rate of Return (IRR), and the payback period? How does the change financial impact our shareholders, customers, employees, and competition? What will be the stakeholders' reaction? What are the contingencies? What are the quantifiable business objectives?

Communications

We have all heard the phrase, "It is impossible to overcommunicate." You will need to develop (or hire) a proficient level of communication to successfully implement ABC/M. It takes nine times (nine, nine, nine, nine, nine, nine, nine, nine, nine) to get the message across for change. Communication is an oft-overlooked portable skill that is refined during ABM implementations.

A large part of communications involves knowing how you, as the sender, connect with the recipient of the communication. Whether you use the Situation, Complication, Resolution structure for your persuasive arguments or some other method, you need to make the communication resonate with the recipient: "What's in it for me?" (WIIFM). Work on connecting with their hearts as well as their minds.

Lastly, since the ABC/M initiative requires strong executive sponsorship, the communications will be corporate-wide (or area-wide) and reach the top levels of executive management. Therefore, ABC/M communications will give some ABC/M team members the opportunity to hone their executive presence and communications.

Goal Alignment

As emphasized several times throughout this book, control and accountability misalignment is the number one problem observed in repeated improvement efforts (ABC/M and other). Recognizing and resolving these misalignments is a portable skill that, unfortunately, you will need to use over and over again. Oftentimes, compensation and incentive plans are not aligned with the best interest of the shareholder. In these cases, compensation and incentive plans are not only part of the problem, they *are* the problem.

As an example of goal misalignment impacts, remember the meltdown of the mortgage business. Mortgage brokers and many top executives were compensated to sell—regardless of the quality and long-term repercussions of the deal. Shareholders and taxpayers were left holding the bag for this major misalignment. Recognizing and implementing changes to this compensation structure would have saved trillions of dollars and years of anguish throughout the world.

Execution

Let's be crystal clear—execution does not mean making PowerPoint presentations. Many internal and external consultants rightly get a bad reputation by showing up, analyzing the current and future states, producing a beautiful "final deliverable" presentation containing observations and recommendations. By the time of the presentation, this final deliverable has not improved the bottom line at all. Even if the information in the presentation is 100 percent accurate, the shareholder value of this document is actually negative. The presentation is an *investment* of time and money in concepts yet to be implemented. It represents the beginning of a long and difficult journey, not a final deliverable.

The ability to drive results to the bottom line is not a commodity. It is a rarity. This is unfortunate for the business world, but fortunate for those employees who really can improve the bottom line. ABC/M will focus you to sharpen your execution ability. By its very nature, ABC is just better information and has no value without execution. You must use the ABC data through ABM to make any ABC/M effort worthwhile.

ADJACENT CAREERS

Because of the high number of portable skills developed while implementing ABC/M, the ABC/M team members will have many career options open to them. Clearly, if they enjoy the job and continue to drive improvements, the option to stay within the ABC/M team is available. Also, if they believe ABC/M cannot be taken any further at the company, they will have ABC/M implementation options elsewhere. Both of these paths result in deeper knowledge and experience: They may be on their way to becoming ABC/M gurus.

Sometimes, though, a team member is not passionate about ABC/M, or is hungry to learn other skills. There are many adjacent jobs for experienced ABC/M team members. Work with those ABC/M team members who are looking to change careers to help them obtain valuable, portable experience for their desired next step. They will not enter as experts in these adjacent careers, but they will have some

FIGURE 8.1 ABC/M Career Adjacencies

relevant experience. Their ABC/M experience may open opportunities and will assist in the transition.

Figure 8.1 highlights some of the possible adjacent careers available to ABC/M team members. Figure 8.2 shows that the majority of ABC/M portable skills apply to each of the adjacent career possibilities. The rest of this section discusses those careers.

Product Manager

Product managers are responsible for planning, delivery, and profitability of products at all stages of the product life cycle. Additionally,

ABC/M Portable Skills

Adjacent Careers	Product Profitability	Customer Segmentation and Profitability	Project Planning	Organizational Change Management	Project Prioritization and Portfolio Management	Process Improvement	Business Case Development	Communications	Goal Alignment	Execution
Product Manager	✓		✓	✓	✓	✓	✓	✓	✓	✓
Customer Segment Analyst		✓	✓	✓	✓	✓	✓	✓	✓	✓
Pricing Manager	✓	✓	✓			✓	✓	✓	✓	✓
Project Manager			✓	✓		✓	✓	✓	✓	✓
Program Manager			✓	✓	✓	✓	✓	✓	✓	✓
Process Improvement Consultant			✓	✓	✓	✓	✓	✓	✓	✓
Financial Analyst	✓	✓	✓		✓	✓	✓	✓	✓	✓
Communications Manager			✓	✓		✓		✓	✓	✓

FIGURE 8.2 Adjacent Careers—ABC/M Portable Skills Matrix

product managers are often responsible for product marketing. ABC/M team members can utilize their experience analyzing product profitability, recommending improvements, and driving improved margins to transition into product manager roles. Remember, it is not uncommon for product managers to be evaluated and rewarded on revenue and revenue growth instead of profitability and margin growth. In these situations, the ABC/M team may have more experience improving margins than the current product managers.

Customer Segment Analyst

Customer segment analysts create and examine groups of people sharing common characteristics that cause them to have similar product needs or to behave in a similar manner. A customer segment has needs and behaviors distinct from other segments, has common needs and behaviors within its own segment, and it responds similarly to stimuli (marketing campaigns, pricing changes, etc.). Customer segmentation results within financial services feed pricing elasticity models which identify profit margin improvement opportunities.

Pricing Manager

Pricing managers are responsible for maximizing profitability based on the product offer and market conditions (charge what the market will bear). More recently, as indicated above, pricing managers are responsible for maximizing profit by customer segment based on the product offer. This requires extensive and ongoing customer segment pricing elasticity analysis. Therefore, pricing managers look externally to analyze market forces and internally to analyze customer segment reactions to pricing changes.

Project Manager

Project managers are responsible for planning, organizing, and managing resources, timing, and scope to successfully deliver project goals (requirements). As stated throughout this book, strong project management skills are necessary for the successful delivery of the ABC project and the subsequent ABM improvement projects. Like the other adjacent careers, project management expertise requires education and experience. If you elect to pursue a career in project management, take a few project management courses and become a Project Management Professional (PMP).

Program Manager

Program managers are responsible for managing several related projects. Strong program management skills are necessary for the project portfolio management and delivery required in the ABM portion of the ABC/M implementation. It is important to recognize that a great project manager will not necessarily be a great program manager. This is similar to the fact that great first line managers do not necessarily become great middle and senior managers. Program management frequently involves bigger-picture thinking and the ability to manage project managers.

Process Improvement Consultant

Process improvement consultants identify, analyze, and change existing processes within an organization to meet improvement objectives in quality, cycle time, and costs. Process improvement consultants come in many flavors, but can be broken down into two primary types: methodologists and generalists.

Methodologists follow a specific methodology or strategy to deliver successful results. Popular and proven process improvement methodologies include Six Sigma and Total Quality Management (TQM). On the other hand, generalists attempt to select improvement methodologies based on the situation at hand to deliver successful results. While both approaches have pros and cons, both have been used for decades with success.

Regardless, if you choose to become a methodologist or a generalist, make certain to immerse yourself in at least one process improvement methodology. For example, attend Six Sigma training, deliver improvements based on Six Sigma, and become a certified black belt.

Financial Analyst

Financial analysts often include ABC team members. They are responsible for budgeting and forecasting within the organization. In most financial services organizations, financial analysts are responsible for variance analysis, which consists of comparing budget and forecast numbers to actual results and then providing a variance explanation. Also, financial analysts assist in the creation of business cases for projects and validate project results post-implementation. In more progressive companies, financial analysts also identify and track financial improvement opportunities.

Communications Manager

Communications managers plan, implement, monitor, and revise information on all communication channels within an organization and between organizations, including communications to the customers. Communications managers develop corporate communication strategies, design internal and external communications directives, and manage the flow of information, including online communication.

IN CONCLUSION

Activity-Based Costing is an extremely versatile and powerful tool used to improve processes and margins. However, without the bottom line results driven by a disciplined Activity-Based Management program, the investment in the ABC implementation is wasted. Unfortunately, many financial services companies implemented ABC and did not fully comprehend the ABM commitment required to achieve the desired return on the ABC investments. Many of these companies were disappointed and mistakenly blamed ABC for the lack of results. However, the real failure of these implementations was overlooking and undercommitting to the ABM effort necessary to achieve the expected bottom-line results.

Like many organizationally complex improvement initiatives, ABC/M is difficult to implement well. However, the benefit of implementing world-class improvement techniques such as ABC/M remains large. Because of the large potential, organizations will continue to return to ABC/M, hoping for improved results. But consider yourself forewarned—failed ABC/M implementations will fail again unless organizational, methodological, and process changes are made to ensure that the ABC results are used, improvements are made, and changes stick. As Albert Einstein famously stated, "Insanity is doing the same thing over and over again and expecting different results."

Hopefully, this book provides some guidance and encouragement for first-time ABC/M implementers, as well as ABC/M re-implementers. For the ABC/M re-implementers, closely examine your own organization

to determine the reasons for the less-than-stellar previous implementation. Create your own personalized list of lessoned learned
and potentially repeated pitfalls. From the first day of the re-imple-
mentation, incorporate mitigating actions to these pitfalls. A former
professor of mine passed along a quote from an admiral friend of
his: "Don't blame a person for accidentally shooting himself in the
foot. Only blame him if he reloads." Learn from past shortcomings
and adjust your current course. When implemented properly, the
ABC/M benefits are certainly worth the efforts.

ABC Model and Cost Object Reporting Rules and Assumptions

I t is important to set ground rules early in the ABC implementation. This includes high-level ABC model and output rules and assumptions. Since the outputs—particularly the cost object reports—are defined early in the project, it is important to create the ground rules for the outputs first. This section contains an example of rules set within the first month of an ABC implementation at an Information Technology Shared Services organization.

MODELING RULES AND ASSUMPTIONS

Zero Profit Model

The intent of the model is to drive all Shared Services expenses to the appropriate Business Units (BUs). Shared Services also consumes their own resources, but these expenses will be re-assigned to BUs. This re-assignment will be driven to BUs based on their overall Shared Services consumption. The re-assignment will be a single line item on the consumption report.

Activity Relevance

Only activities requiring a minimum of five full-time equivalents (FTEs) or a monthly cost of $40,000 will be used in the costing model. While detailed information regarding most activities will be available using the Planview information, this information will be rolled up for ABC purposes. This modeling rule provides detailed costing information without dropping below managerially relevant information.

E-mail, Meetings, and Other Micro Tasks

E-mail, meetings, and similar micro tasks crossing multiple activities are not listed as tasks within any activity. Any time spent on these types of tasks should be logged to the associated activity. For example, if an e-mail was drafted, sent, or read to surface design problems during an application development project, this time is logged to Design within the application development activities.

Application Development (AD) Lifecycle Terminology

ABC terminology is used in the ABC model and consumption reporting. ABC terminology is common throughout industry and business functions. The ABC model summarizes the current AD Lifecycle for performance and consumption information. A mapping of AD Life cycle modules to ABC Activities was created to bridge time tracking to the ABC Model. AD Lifecycle is specific to IT developers and managers. While AD Lifecycle is appropriate for project development and management within Shared Services, it is too complex for BU reporting.

Depreciation

Some ABC models recalculate the expected useful life of equipment and use this schedule (rather than the accounting depreciation schedule) as the model expense schedule. However, since the Shared Services model needs to tie actual expenses to the general ledger, actual depreciation is driven through the model.

Metrics and Surrogate Drivers

In some cases, ideal drivers (resource or activity) are not available or easily used. In such cases, surrogate drivers may be used to assign consumption costs. Surrogate drivers are readily available, easy to use, and provide directionally correct assignments. Future enhancements of the model include automated use of ideal drivers.

International Costs

As an international corporation, Company XYZ recognizes expenses in several foreign currencies. The foreign currency information is recorded in the general ledger in the local foreign currency. The model requires a foreign exchange (FX) table to convert the foreign currencies to USD. The FX table will be used monthly to convert the general ledger data. The consumption reports will be generated in USD.

COST OBJECT REPORTING RULES AND ASSUMPTIONS

Expected Cost Determination

The expected costs for the model will be determined using FY08 cost data and either FY08 or estimated FY09 drivers. Using a full year to determine standard costs removes monthly fluctuations that affect a full-year extrapolation of a single month's cost/drivers.

Reconciliation for Over/Under Recovery

As with all standard costing systems, there is some monthly variance. The variance can be due to actual cost or volume fluctuations. Since Shared Services is a zero profit Line of Business (LOB), adjustments need to be made as necessary. Over/under recovery will be reconciled on a quarterly basis as a line item on the consumption report.

Premium and Incentive Pricing

To influence consumption, some standard costs may be priced higher (premium priced) to discourage consumption, or priced lower (incentive priced) to encourage consumption. Premium and incentive pricing are used sparingly in the initial consumption report development.

Cost Object Dimensions

Activity consumption can be viewed in three dimensions: BU organization, product, and customer. Using multidimensional modeling and reporting tools, all dimensions can be viewed. BUs are combined to form LOBs.

Capitalized Projects

As projects are capitalized in accordance with SOP-98, they will not be expensed to the BUs. There is a section on the BU consumption report which itemizes capitalized project expenditures. These capitalized expenditures are for informational and planning purposes only. Amortized software is itemized, expensed, and billed on the BU invoice.

BU Consumption Reporting

Initial consumption reports will be generated for each LOB and later generated by BU reporting. By providing BU consumption reports, Shared Services will realize the primary objective of BU consumption control. The BU invoices can be mapped to Legal Entities for profitability reporting and transfer pricing.

Mapping Projects/Applications to BUs and Platforms

It is assumed that Shared Services maintains a mapping of all applications and projects to BUs. It is also assumed that Shared Services maintains (or will maintain) a mapping of all applications and projects to platforms. These mappings are essential to determine BU consumption and total platform costs.

Index